AF473964

Pierre Bonnard
and his dogs

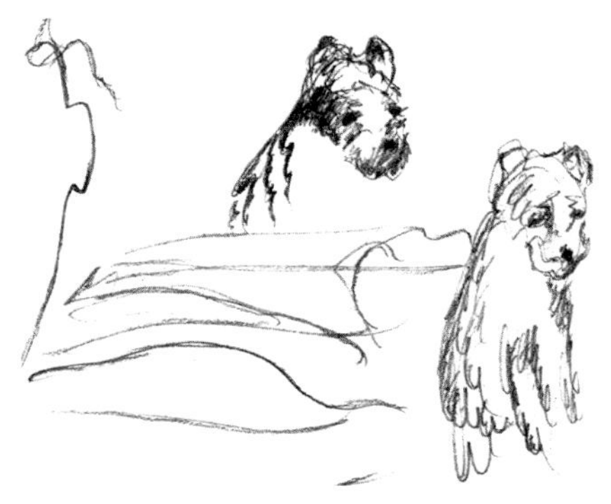

Amigos Forever
Collection directed
by Martin Bethenod

Stéphane Guégan

Pierre Bonnard
and his dogs

Norma éditions

Preface

Martin Bethenod

The publication of *Pierre Bonnard and his Dogs* by Stéphane Guégan provides an ideal opportunity to clear up a misunderstanding that sometimes hangs over the “Amigos Forever” series, of which this is the fourth installment.

This series, launched in 2024 with *Picasso* by Jean-Louis Andral, explores the relationships between artists and the dogs present in both their lives and their works, but in no way is it tainted by any anti-feline speciesism. On the contrary, it seeks to dispel the persistent cliché that claims cats and dogs to be age-old enemies, where loving one species or the other should be an exclusive—and sometimes even a contentious—affair. Let us proclaim it loud and clear: cats and dogs have an equal right to human affection and to be present in artworks—a presence which is often concurrent, as is attested by the long history of painting, from Titian (*Pilgrims at Emmaus*) to Marguerite Gérard (*L’Élève intéressante*). Pierre Bonnard provided eminent examples of this joint presence, from *Femmes au Jardin* (1890–1891, see pp. 22—23) to *L’Après-midi bourgeoise* (1900, see pp. 40—41), as was shown in the splendid exhibition “Entre chiens et chats, Bonnard et l’animalité,” conceived in 2016 for the Musée Bonnard in Le Cannet by its director, Véronique Serrano.

Although this book focuses primarily on dogs, it never overlooks the fact that Bonnard’s paintings feature over a hundred cats, ever-present in his interiors, and that the artist himself had a dual spirit, a canine and feline polarity, by which he went from “cat-like dream-filled intermissions [to] sleep between bursts of exaltation typical of dogs,” as can be read in a note he wrote in the margins of his diary in 1944.

The antagonism between cats and dogs was created by humans. It is a fabrication, a popular belief, most aptly criticized in the first issue of *Le Canard sauvage* in 1913, in a type of plate not yet known as a "bande dessinée," titled *Soleil de printemps*. Under drawings of cats and dogs represented in various poses, the following text could be read: "The spring sun is shining... Enemy races are sleeping side by side. Friendly races show interest in one another. Humans seek inspiration from them. The friendly races increase their show of interest." These words prefigured what 21st-century philosophers such as Donna Haraway, in her *Manifesto* from 2003, and Vinciane Despret (*Quand le loup habitera avec l'agneau*, 2002) would call "companion species." They were by Alfred Jarry, and the images were by Pierre Bonnard.

The friendly collaboration between both men, which dated back to the turn of the 20th century—when Bonnard illustrated the *Almanach illustré du Père Ubu* in 1901—if not earlier, continued after Jarry's death in 1907: as a tribute to the writer, Bonnard gave the name "Ubu" to the dachshund he always kept by his side, and whose silhouette found its way into countless drawings. Years later, the writer Roger Grenier chose not to give the same name to his own dog, after the Collège de Pataphysique informed him that "it would be disrespectful." There is a delightful irony in the name Ubu being associated with the notion of respect.

Dogs' names are a subject for history (Peritas, gifted to Alexander the Great by Alexander I, King of Epirus, also known as "The Molossian"), literary history (Paul-Jean Toulet's charming, irresistible poem "My dog was named Tom, my bitch was named Djaly. More pompous names deserved to be forgotten by history"), and art history (models by Oudry and Desportes, whose portraits show the name in golden capital letters; Hockney's, Warhol's, and Picasso's dachshunds; not to mention *Martin* (1879) by Rosa Bonheur). While the names of few of Bonnard's cats have been remembered, the names of his and his family's dogs are well known.

More than "theatrical names," to borrow a phrase by Lévi-Strauss, who devoted several pages to the subject in *Tristes tropiques*, the names of Bonnard's companions were, in various ways, literary names. Aside from Ubu, already mentioned, let us cite Poucette (the French name for Thumbelina, from Andersen's tale), Black—one of Léautaud's dogs would bear the same name—, and Bella, who belonged to his sister Andrée and announced Giraudoux's eponymous novel. There was also Ravageau, a name similar to Ravager from Kipling's *Dog Stories*. Stéphane Guégan, wide reader that he is, deftly emphasizes the importance of Bonnard's relationship with texts and their authors, as well as the place occupied by dogs in his relationship with Verlaine, Jules Renard, and Octave Mirbeau.

I would like to add a further name to this list, that of an artist whose talent for describing dogs—and making them talk—is unrivaled in the entire 20th century. For instance, on the subject of dachshunds, a race much beloved by Bonnard, she describes them as "omniscient braggarts." Could anyone have put it better? Her name is Colette. Not only because her book *Belles saisons* from 1947 was illustrated with six drawings by Bonnard, but above all because some of Colette's texts read like literary transcriptions of paintings Bonnard could have made. Let us read the first words from some chapters of *Dialogues de bêtes*, which began to be published in 1904: "Front steps in the sun. Napping after lunch. Toby-Chien and Kiki-la-Doucette are lying on the scorched stones. A Sunday silence..."

Or, further on: "A bedroom in the countryside. An autumn sun shining through lowered blinds. She is stretched out in a white woolen dress on a chaise longue, apparently asleep. Kiki-la-Doucette is grooming herself on a narrow console; Toby-Chien watches, lying in a sphinx position on the rug, right by Her, heeding the words of his master who is tiptoeing out of the room."

Doesn't it feel like we're in a painting?

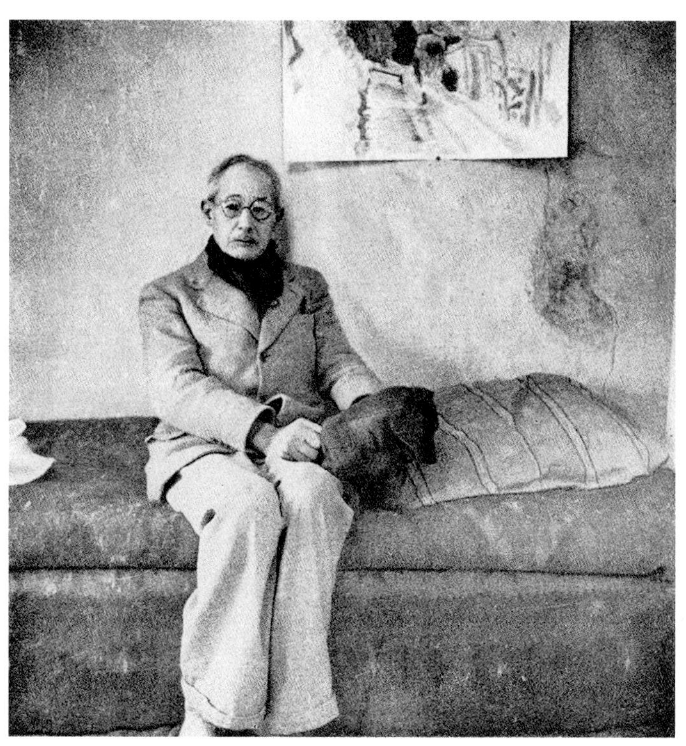

In memory of Ulysses

Could this be the last photograph of Pierre Bonnard? Who can say? Thadée Natanson, author of the snapshot, claimed as much when he published it, adding the date 1947—the year of his friend's death. The two had been very close ever since their rollicking years at *La Revue blanche*, and here they seem to be bidding farewell to each other. Bonnard had opened his door, his studio with its cracked walls, and his frugal private life to Cartier-Bresson in early 1944, and to Brassaï and Gisèle Freund during the summer of 1946. To his great friend Thadée, he left a final image, one that could extend, for all eternity, a meeting with no tomorrow. Although the old master's expression seems to hover between sadness and weariness, his eyes show no sign of distress. They are staring straight at the camera, piercing us viewers. His house in Le Cannet had never looked more like Fra Angelico's cell, and Bonnard like an aged Chinese or Japanese calligrapher, at peace with his non-ego. Besides, his dandyish clothes—buttoned jacket, large scarf—rule out any notion of death, temporarily circumvented each day by the joy of painting. As for the dachshund by his side, he is looking away. Why would Bonnard impose on animals a stricter discipline than the one governing his own painting, itself an equal blend of order and feeling?

Page 8

Thadée Natanson, *Pierre Bonnard*, 1947

I appreciate the quiet independence of the little dog, who isn't sitting up to beg, and I like the fact that the master didn't ask his companion of old age to pose. This photograph, published in Thadée's book in 1951, has since become a kind of testimonial. Could it be considered to encapsulate Bonnard's style, full of gaps and latencies? Yes. And seen as a definitive emblem of his relationship with canines, strangers to human arrogance? Yes.

Bonnard on all fours

Forty years separate this photograph from another one, much better known today. The year is 1908, the address 60 Rue de Douai on the edge of the Batignolles neighborhood, a former Impressionist stronghold. Bonnard is in his place. Count Henry Kessler notes that there was an abandoned convent there, where an eccentric Bonnard decided to set up his studio. The decoration was already extremely sparse, but to deprive himself of dogs would have been too much. They had been his childhood companions, always running between his legs, putting zest into his life, reminding him that joy, loyalty, and discipline formed its backbone. The photographs from 1908 say it better than words, especially as in this case the roles are inverted. One shows Bonnard crouched down, wearing a creased suit and Belle Époque ankle boots, in conversation with a splendidly lanky and hairy spaniel named Black. Like dog, like man. The viewer is immediately seized by the dog's eyes, two specks of light inside a black mask. Black was the life of a party, as confirmed in another snapshot taken during the same session but less frequently reproduced.

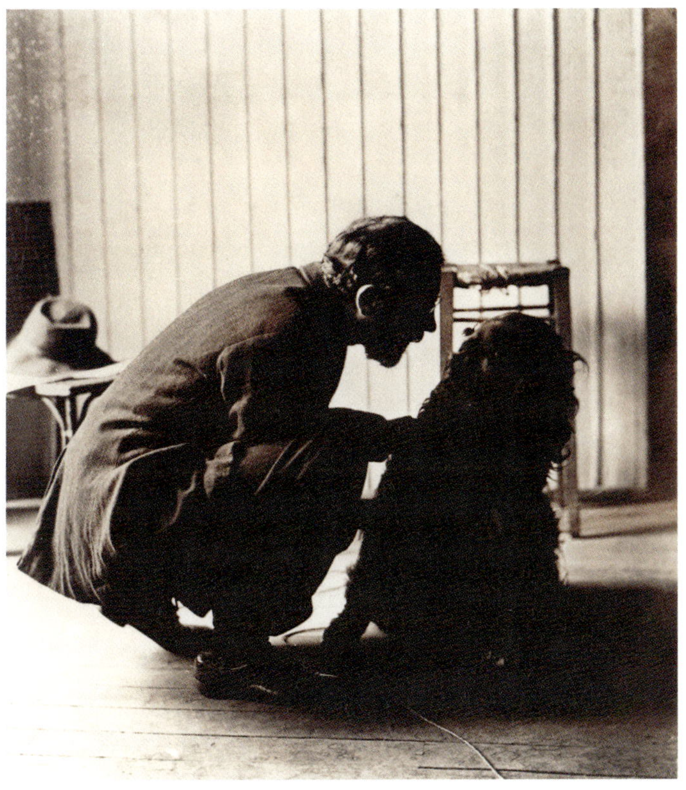

Anonymous, *Pierre Bonnard et son chien dans l'atelier de la rue de Douai*, circa 1908. Le Cannet, Musée Bonnard

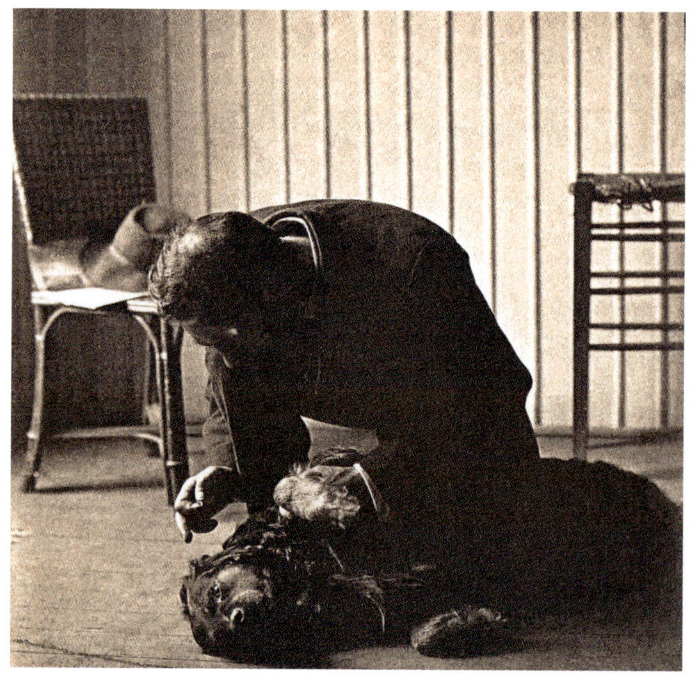

Anonymous, *Pierre Bonnard et son chien dans l'atelier de la rue de Douai*, circa 1908. Le Cannet, Musée Bonnard

It suggests a different story: the painter is hugging Black tightly, as though at one with his dog lying on the studio floor, who is more than pleased to have his stomach stroked and scratched. One would think Bonnard's hands—so beautiful and powerful—had been made to give pleasure to his little doggies, so important to him and, as will soon be seen, to his art. The Kodak he bought for himself at the turn of the 20th century—which signaled a fresh start for him—soon revealed his love of animals. Since Bonnard quickly understood how the emerging cinematograph worked, he allowed himself the luxury of taking a kind of forward tracking shot, in 1898. Another memorable photo has a dog running towards him, while two children smile and watch and a third walks away. Instead of dominating his subjects, the painter lets them take over, adapting to the four protagonists' scale and field of vision. Maurice Denis was right in 1943: out of all the Nabis, Bonnard was the one who refused to age. To separate himself from children and animals.

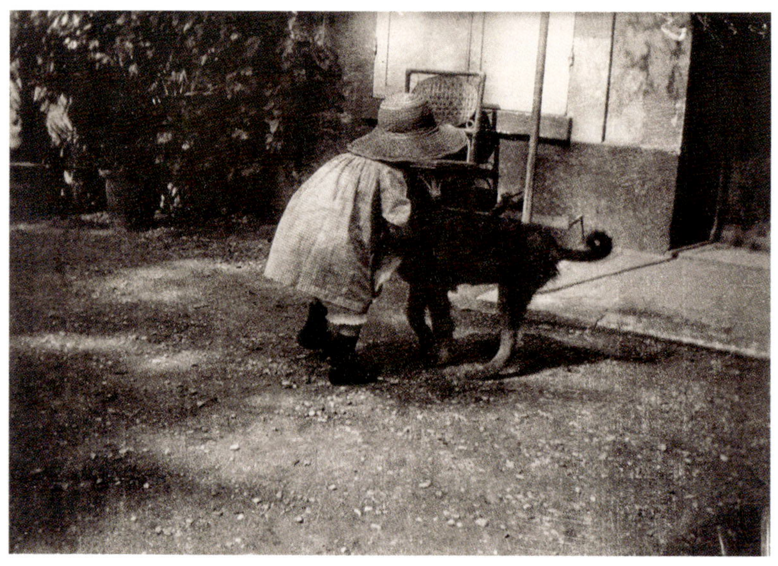

Renée de dos embrassant un chien, 1898.
Paris, Musée d'Orsay

15

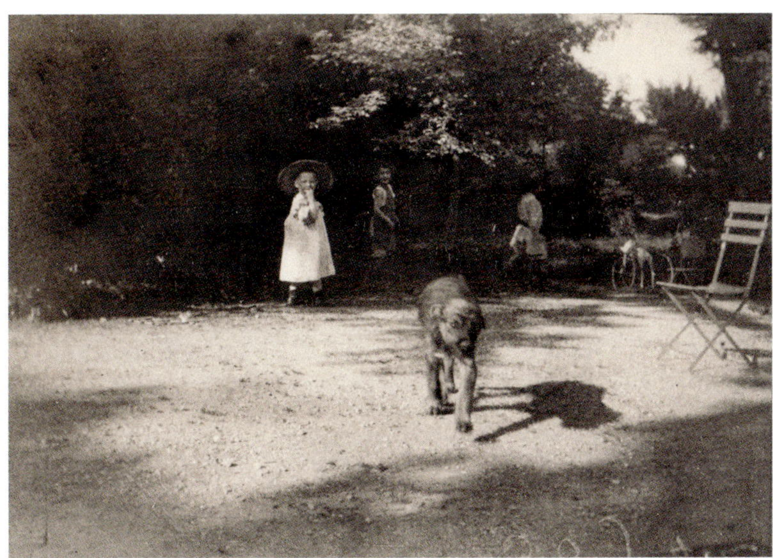

Chiens et enfants, 1898.
Paris, Musée d'Orsay

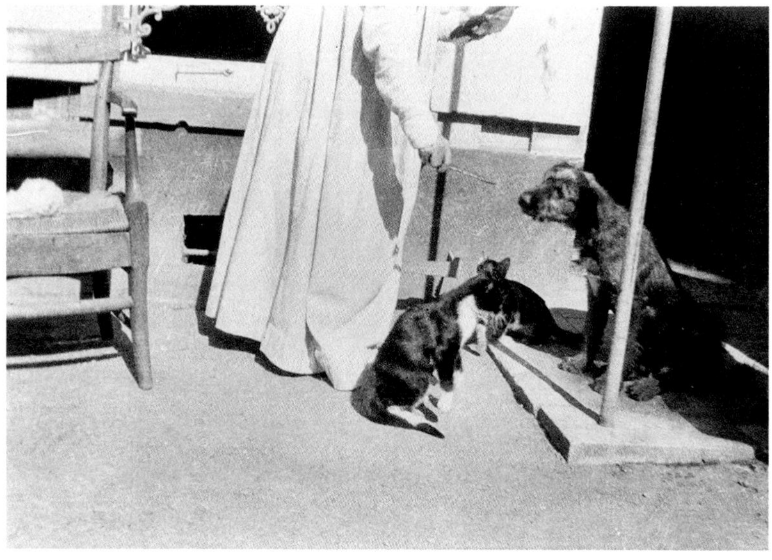

Andrée Terrasse jouant avec deux chats et un chien, undated. Paris, Musée d'Orsay

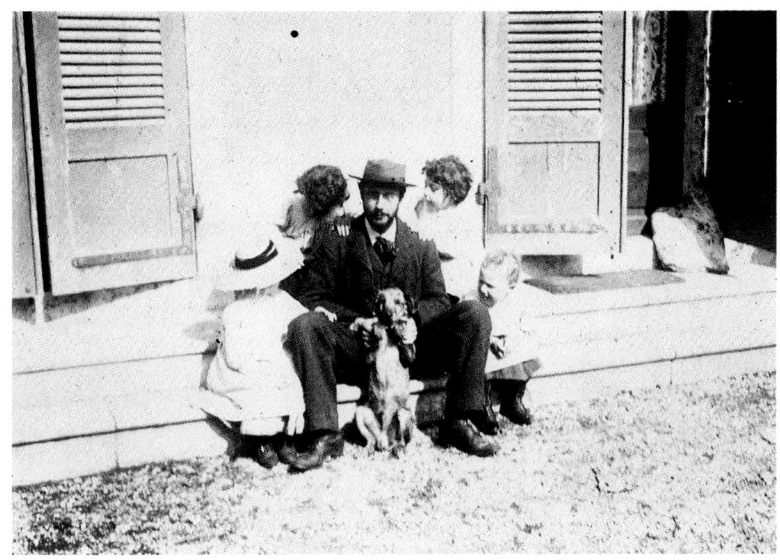

Anonymous, *Pierre Bonnard assis sur le seuil de sa maison avec Renée, Charles, Jean et Robert Terrasse*, circa 1899. Paris, Musée d'Orsay

Bounds and rebounds

Dogs shook up and disrupted his painting in 1890–1891, when the two early masterpieces *Femmes au jardin* and *Deux caniches* came into the world. Under the influence of Émile Bernard, the famous painter and writer from Pont-Aven, art history has tried to persuade us that the Nabi nebula, at its inception, was merely an annex of the Gauguin school and, consequently, a meek offshoot of Symbolism. Although true when applied to Denis, the theory falls apart when considering Bonnard's work at the time. Besides, in 1943, Denis himself recalled the initial resistance of his colleague's "realism" against the harsh lessons of the Breton primitivists. Bonnard was admittedly highly receptive to the novelty of Gauguin's work, as well as to the audacity of Japanese prints. However, this does not make him a mere successor, let alone an old-fashioned illustrator. Instead of stating yet again how often his early works eschew perspective and traditional shapes in favor of surface effects, let us embrace, without restraint, his youthful brushstrokes and their lively arabesques. The depth and movement they suggest rule out all sense of perspective. Bonnard wasn't even twenty-five in 1891, when he appended his monogram to the painting he submitted to the Salon des Indépendants. A true coup de force, the portrait of his sister Andrée, soon to marry the musician Claude Terrasse, is framed in an elegant kakemono format, enlivened by two bouncing dogs, probably Ravageau and Bella, an Irish settler and a spaniel. The first dog is huddled against his mistress, raising his head as she strokes him. Despite the influence of *Japonisme*, the painting reflects a keen observation of real life.

Page 19

Andrée Bonnard et ses chiens, 1898,
oil on canvas, 188 × 90 cm. Private collection

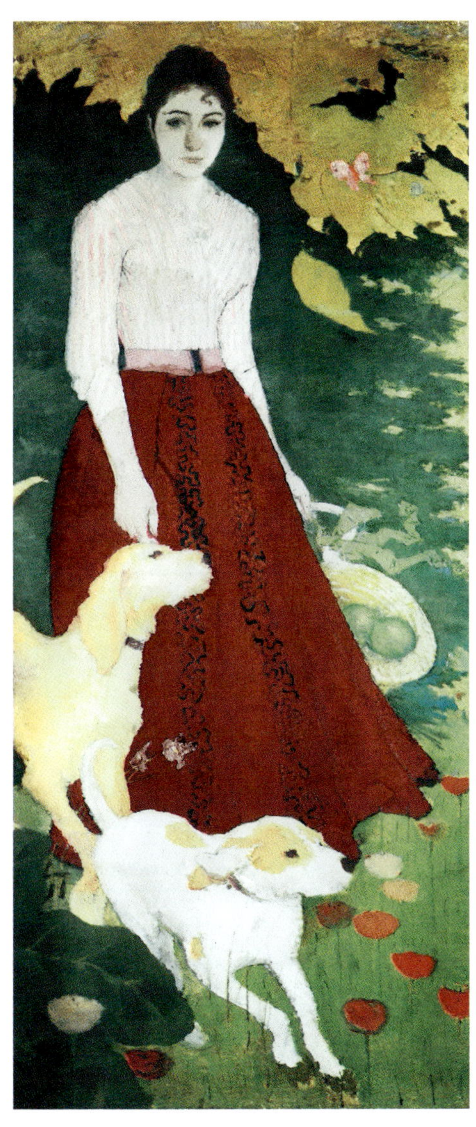

Cavalcades

Prior to 1900, Bonnard had already painted several dogs bounding forwards for the sheer pleasure of it, or out of pure, gratuitous fun. Each work had required eye-popping distortions, as lively as the protagonists themselves. Bonnard's painting, according to the subject he chose, often presented many canine aspects, in which lines and colors combined to form a centrifugal center of energy. The most frenetic of *Femmes au jardin*'s four panels is the one on the left; its movement and explosive verve take the series to a new level, where the screen's planar nature contends with the genre of easel painting. As attested in a letter he sent to his mother, Bonnard decided not to choose between the two, and the resulting ambiguity fits well with the paintings, which make up a whole without sacrificing their own identity. Under wild vegetation, the white dog and the young woman wearing a polka dot dress are rousing each other. For the *France-Champagne* poster (1891), Bonnard had painted his cousin Berthe Schaedlin—a blonde woman from Alsace for whom he had a somewhat romantic attachment—as a sensual mound of foam. Was he identifying with the animal standing on its hindlegs in near-ecstasy? Was he appropriating the dog's vibrant emotion? It's more than likely. *Femmes au jardin* met with success at the Salon des Indépendants, where *Le Bon Chien* was also exhibited, a programmatic title for a painting which may be the famous work now at the Clark Art Institute in Williamstown—at least, I am suggesting the possibility. Represented again are the painter's sister and cousin, decidedly crucial to his pictorial fictions. In the opposite corner, a well-behaved Ravageau is offering his paw. The date and signature have been appended to his frizzy coat, as if Bonnard was once again portraying himself under a guise.

Page 21

Le Bon Chien, 1891, oil on canvas, 41 × 32.5 cm. Williamstown, Clark Art Institute

Pages 22–23

Femmes au jardin, 1890–1891, oil on canvas, 160.5 × 48 cm (for each painting). Paris, Musée d'Orsay

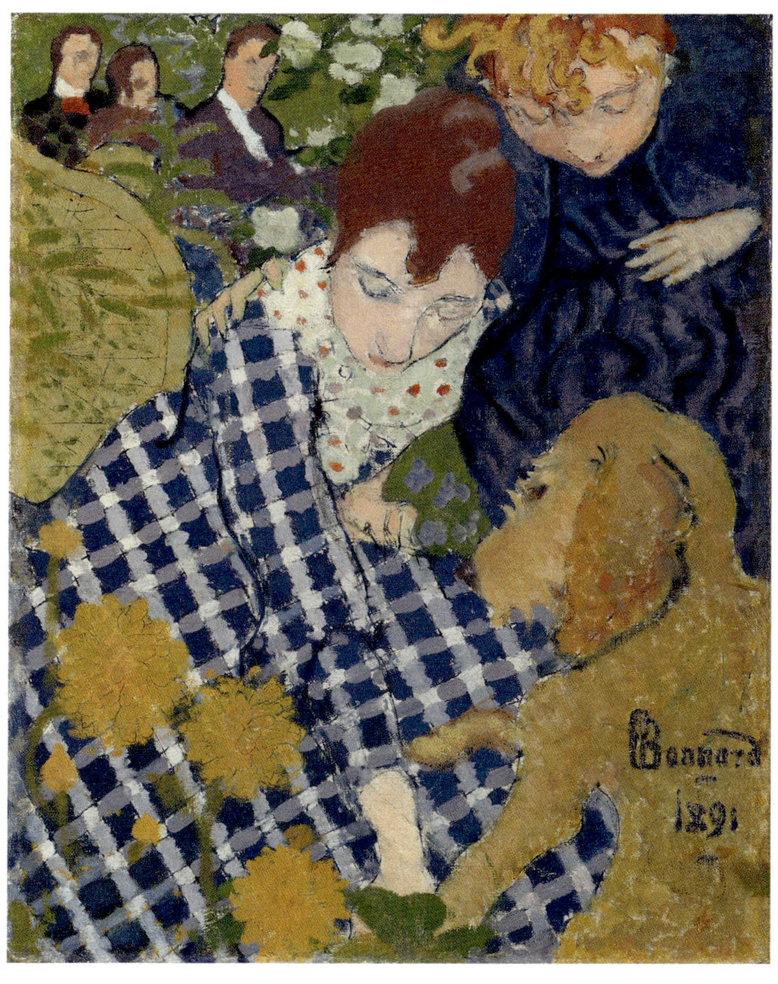
Bonnard
1891

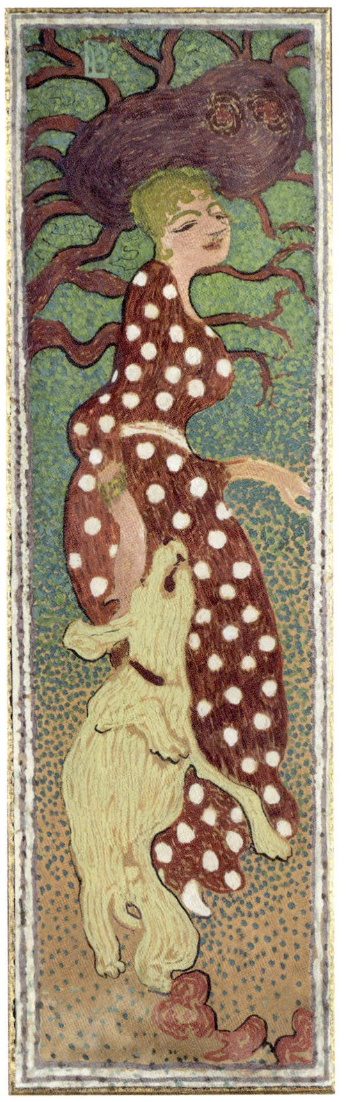

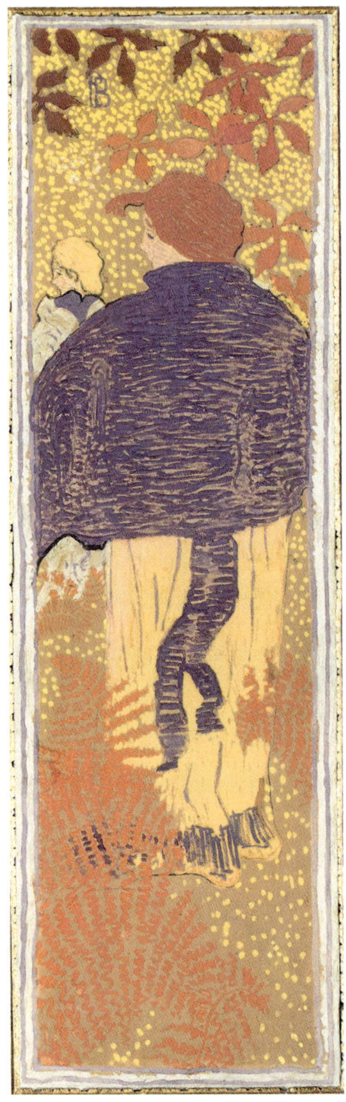

23

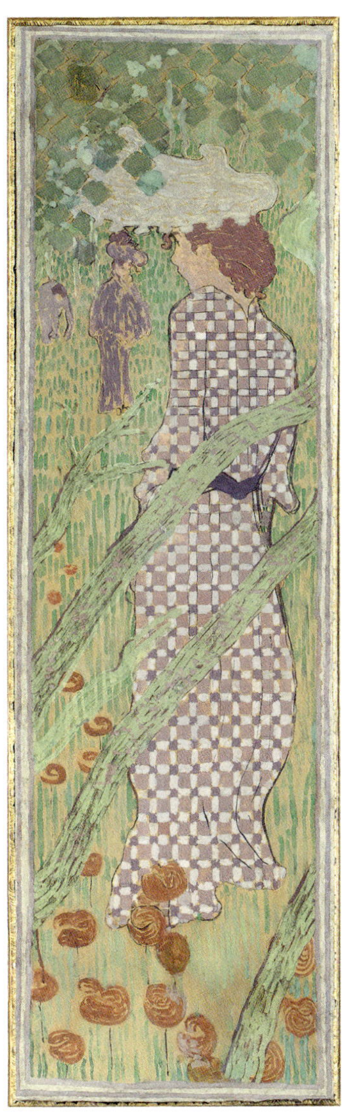

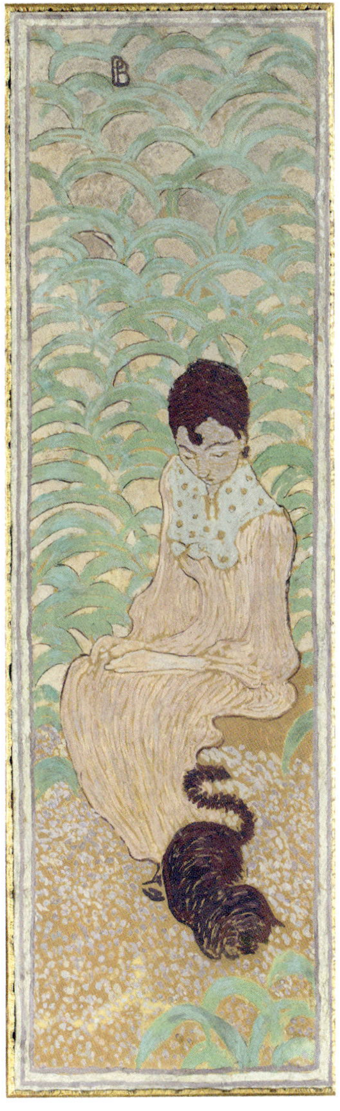

Behind the good-naturedness of the domesticated animal, *Le Bon Chien* could be expressing a less artificial desire for attachment, which would apply to both the dogs and their mistresses. In late 1891, Bonnard took part in a competition organized by the Union Centrale des Arts Décoratifs, predecessor to the Musée des Arts Décoratifs. He failed to win the jury over with his project for Japanese-inspired furniture and arrangements; it was on this occasion, however, that he painted *Deux caniches* and its frenzied round, all the more irresistible for its tight framing, the dogs' momentum driving it to the brink of explosion. With all the protagonists in his compositions, Bonnard liked to put on a show of candidness, lending his paintbrushes to the childish behavior he took pleasure in depicting. Doesn't the green background, alive with fresh spring grass, turn the whirling scene into a vision of childhood paradise? Vuillard was Proustian by sedimentation; Bonnard was Proustian by distraction.

Page 25

Deux caniches, 1891,
oil on canvas, 36.3 × 39.7 cm

Pages 26–27

La Rue. Homme aux prises de deux chiens,
c. 1895, oil on wood, 29,5 x 40 cm.
Private collection

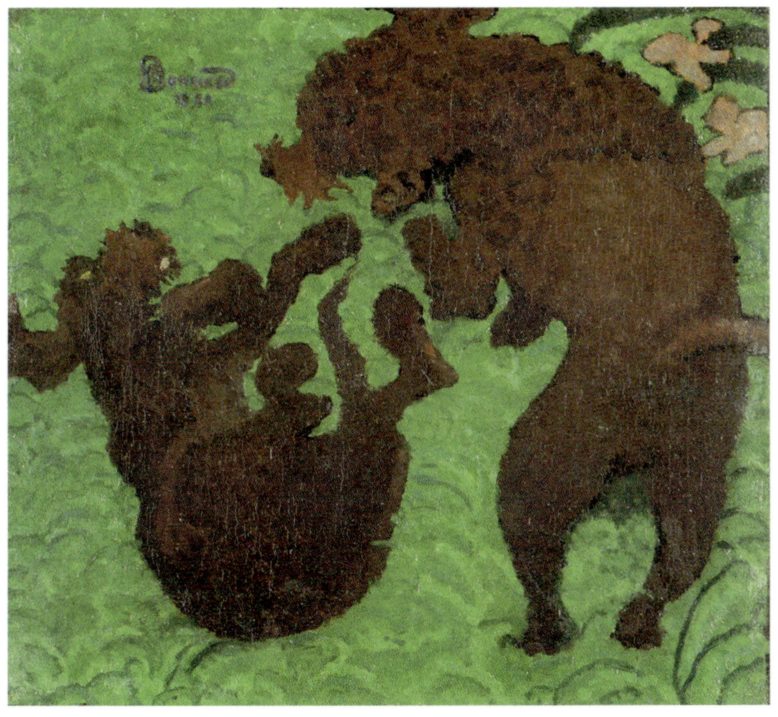

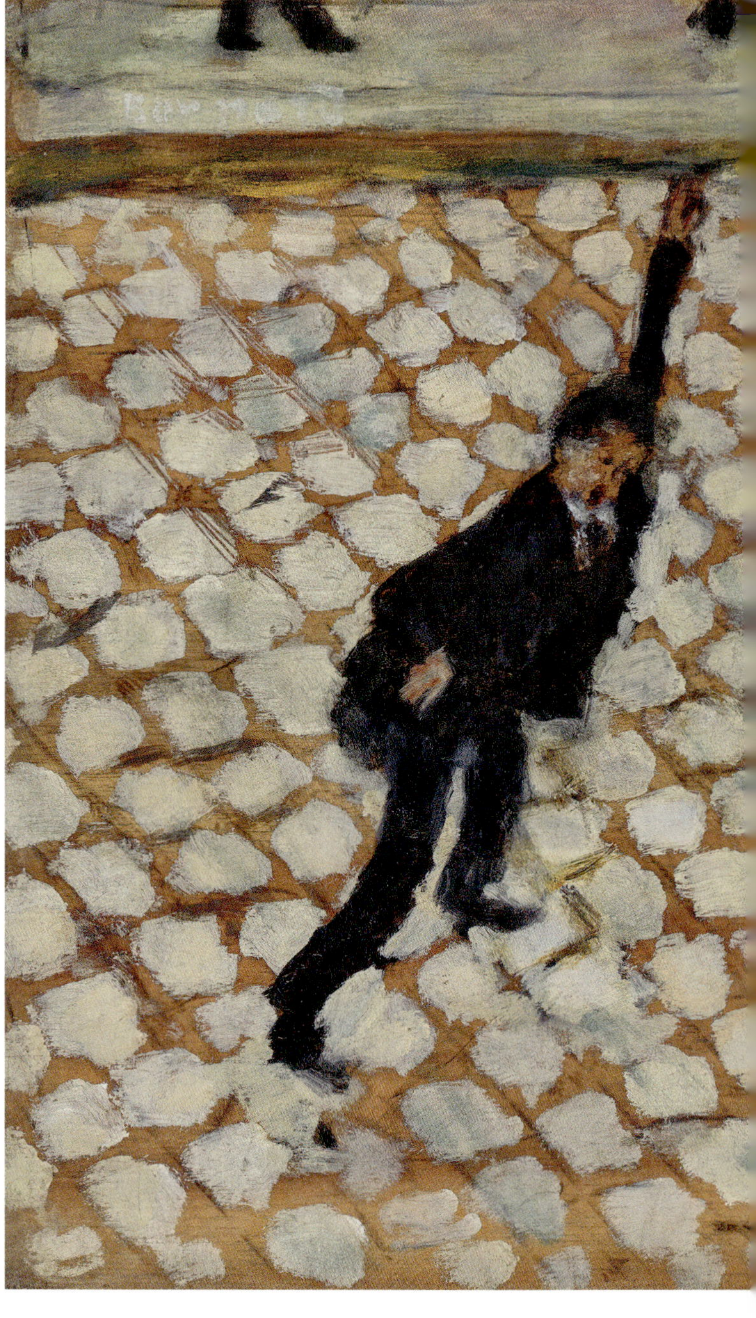

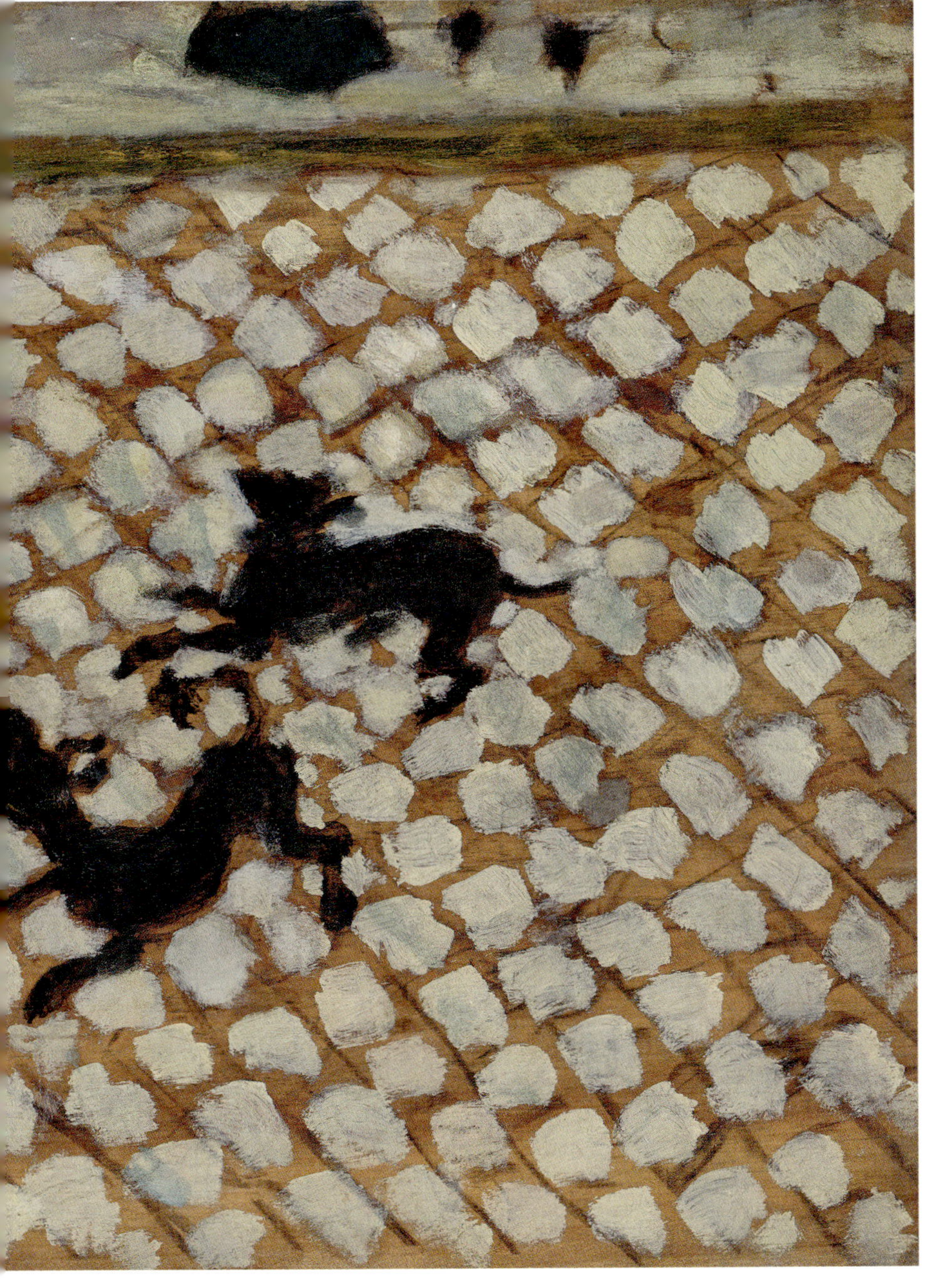

Apparition

Would Bonnard have fallen for Marthe de Méligny, born Maria Boursin, with her humble Berry upbringing, delicate health and mercurial moods, if she hadn't shared his love of dogs? Their meeting around 1893 is still shrouded in a certain mystery, as is their oddly ambiguous relationship, but she did possess an animal quality which was soon captured and exalted by his paintings. Since Bonnard didn't follow the rules and customs of his social environment, he decided he might as well break them. He even gave in to a particular whim of his: to relive the moment he fell in love by doing a series of small paintings where Marthe plays the role of passers-by dressed to the nines, skipping about on the Paris streets, accompanied by equally nimble dogs. The eye can barely make one out in the foreground of the famous painting *L'Omnibus* from 1895, an absolute gem. The painting is deliberately hazy, its slight blurriness conveying the hustle and bustle of city life. Whether Bonnard had seen Japanese woodcuts depicting brothels inhabited by geishas and their canine companions or not, his liberated Parisian women and their appearance could not fail to cause a stir among contemporary viewers. The little dogs held on leashes here and there seem precisely to suggest a certain flightiness, or even a dissoluteness, which doesn't comply with the domestication of immoral thoughts, that bedrock of values instilled in young women from polite society. With its evident kinetic quality, *La Promenade des nourrices* toys with the idea of contrasting collarless dogs with greyhounds confined to their apartments, respectively at the top and the bottom of the screen, just like Balzac often juxtaposed upper and lower urban classes in *La Comédie humaine*.

Page 29

L'Omnibus, 1895, oil on canvas, 59 × 41 cm. Private collection

Pages 30-31

La Promenade des nourrices, 1894, distemper on canvas, 147.3 × 45.1 cm (for each panel). New York, Museum of Modern Art

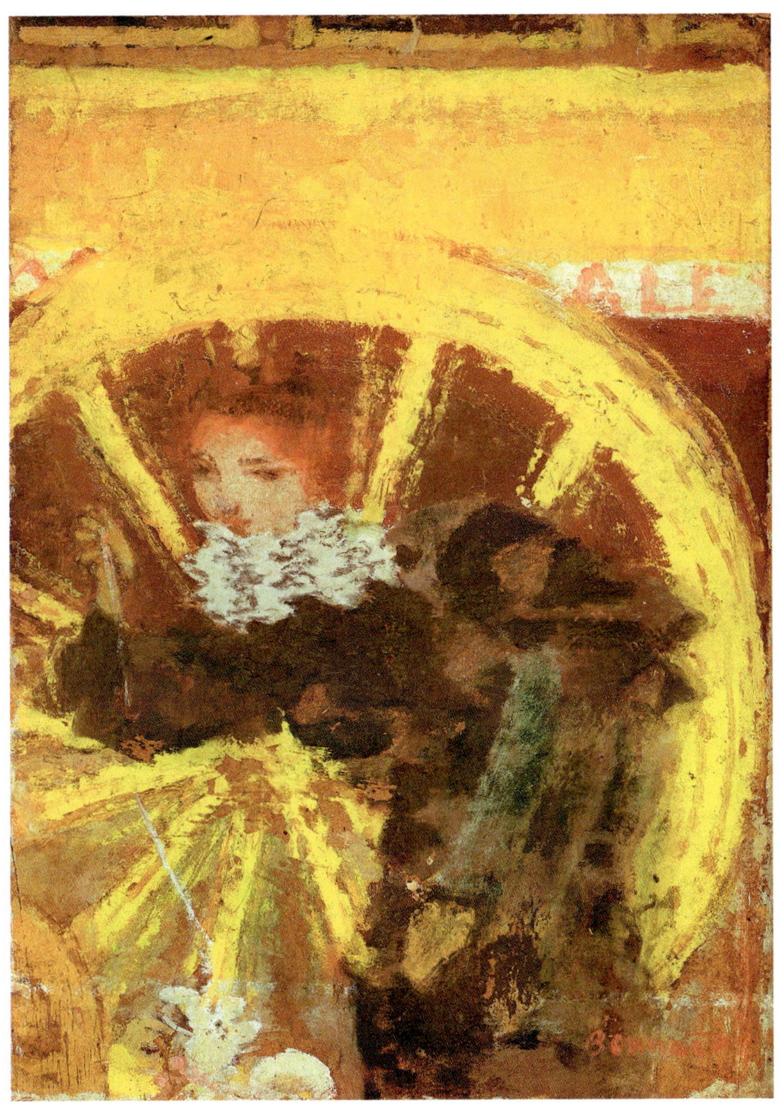

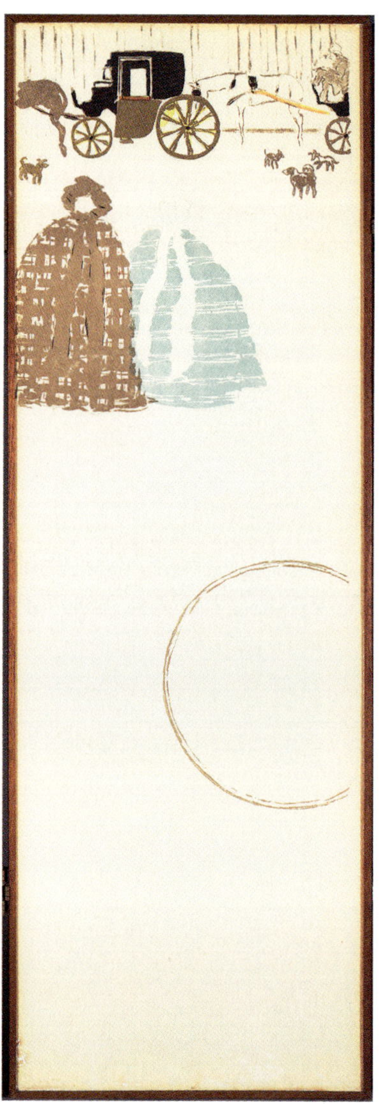

31

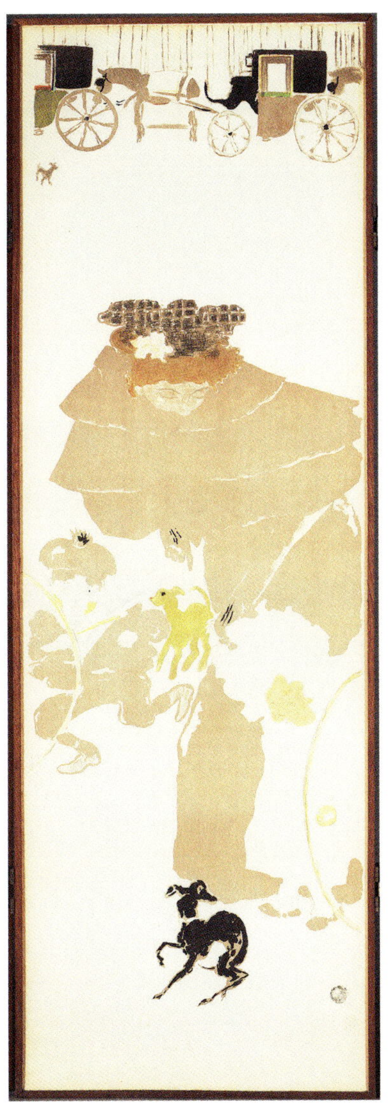

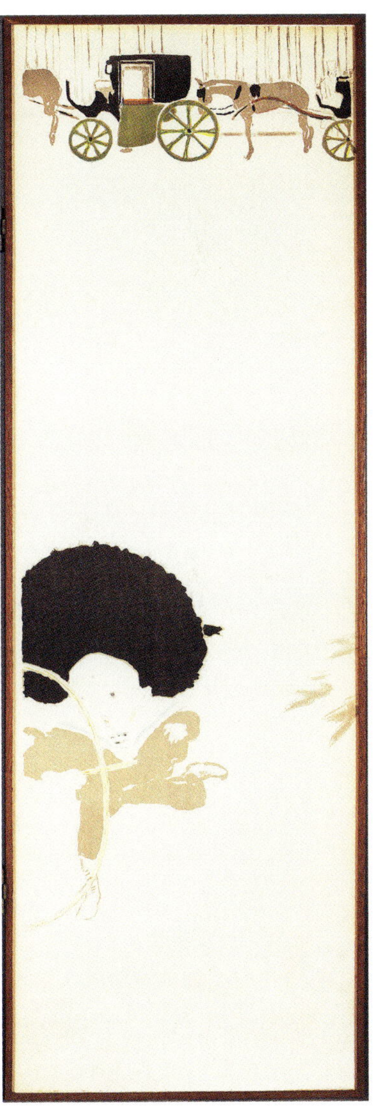

In the description Bonnard wrote to his mother, the theme of social stratification is not only perceptible, but even plainly articulated: “I am painting a screen [...]. The setting is Place de la Concorde, where a young mother is walking past with her children, nannies and dogs. At the top, on the very edge, there is a cab stop. All this is set against an off-white background which closely recalls Place de la Concorde when it is full of dust and looks like a little Sahara.” Humor hasn’t deserted this particular masterpiece.

Wanderings

Similar in that regard to his friend Toulouse-Lautrec, also in the Natansons’ and *La Revue blanche*’s close circle, Bonnard stopped following the rules of his class as soon as he heard the call of the dog begin to resound, like the horn call in *Hernani*. *Une rue à Eragny-sur-Oise* indeed belonged to Thadée Natanson, a great lover of dogs, and was completed the year he began to write about the painter and his unmatched Intimism, which Natanson described as having “the very charm and feeling of real things.” And of real beings, one might add, upon seeing the small painting that rivals urban scenes by Vermeer and Pieter de Hooch. Bonnard was obsessed with the Northern masters. A wheelbarrow, humble dwellings with closed shutters, two dogs—so little yet so much. The two companions, although aware of each other’s presence, aren’t speaking to each other: one is sniffing at something, the other has his nose in the air. The street, humble though it might be, is theirs, and the painting is generously organized around them, situated at their height, following their impenetrable thoughts.

Page 33

Une rue à Éragny-sur-Oise, circa 1894, oil on pressed cardboard, 54.3 × 44 cm. Washington, National Gallery of Art

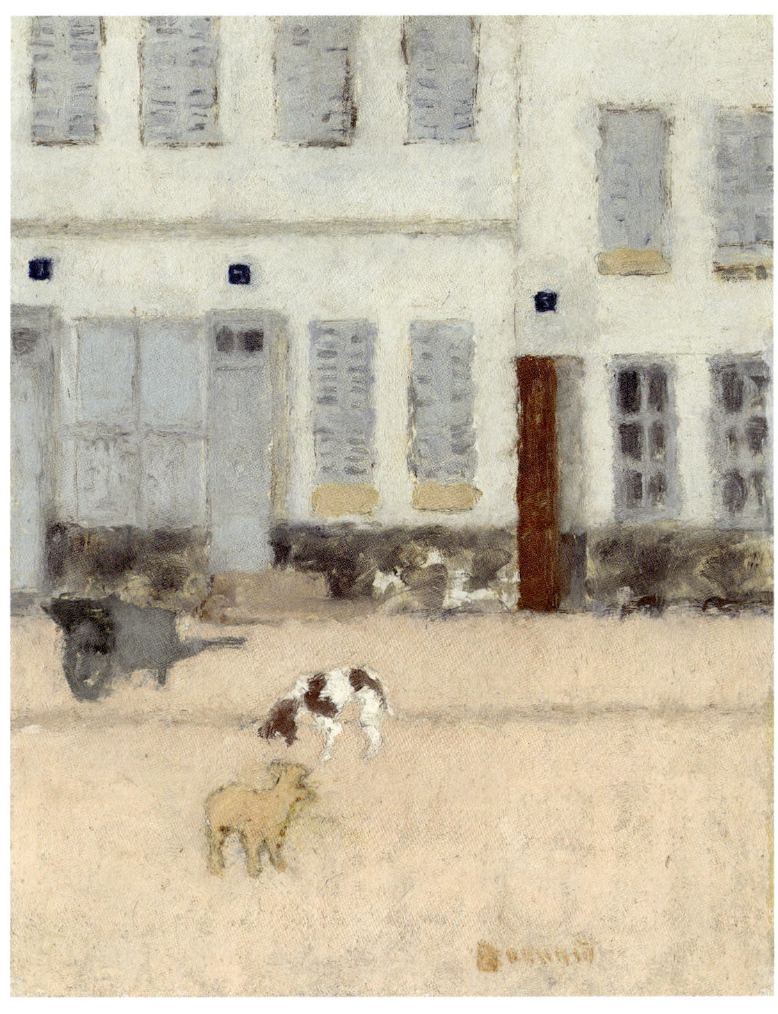

Twenty kilometers away from Paris, the countryside begins. Eragny had 500 inhabitants in the late 19th century, as well as one local celebrity, the naturalist writer Bernardin de Saint-Pierre, who had died there in 1814. Bonnard painting in the footsteps of the author of *Paul et Virginie*, often represented with his dog Fidèle, causes the mind to wander, and does indeed make sense. Both were equally preoccupied with the continuity of the living world, as well as with the idea of a golden age. The loss of Arcadia, the 19th century's great cause for nostalgia, sometimes drove Bonnard to the fringes of social art. *La Petite Blanchisseuse*, a four-color print closely resembling those by the Japanese as well as Lautrec's, features a laundrywoman carrying an oversized basket, but also echoes earlier works by Daumier, as well as the imagery of slave children and the poetry of Montmartre. Social criticism and technical prowess come together. The painter's aim is more clearly visible when comparing the final work to one of its preparatory drawings. The large sheet from the New York Met shows that Bonnard had begun by featuring a trio of passers-by in conversation, above the dog, before deciding to isolate the animal out of fraternal feeling for the little laundrywoman, frail shadow collapsing under the weight of her burden.

Page 35

La Petite Blanchisseuse, 1896, four-color print, 29.3 × 19.6 cm. Paris, Bibliothèque Nationale de France

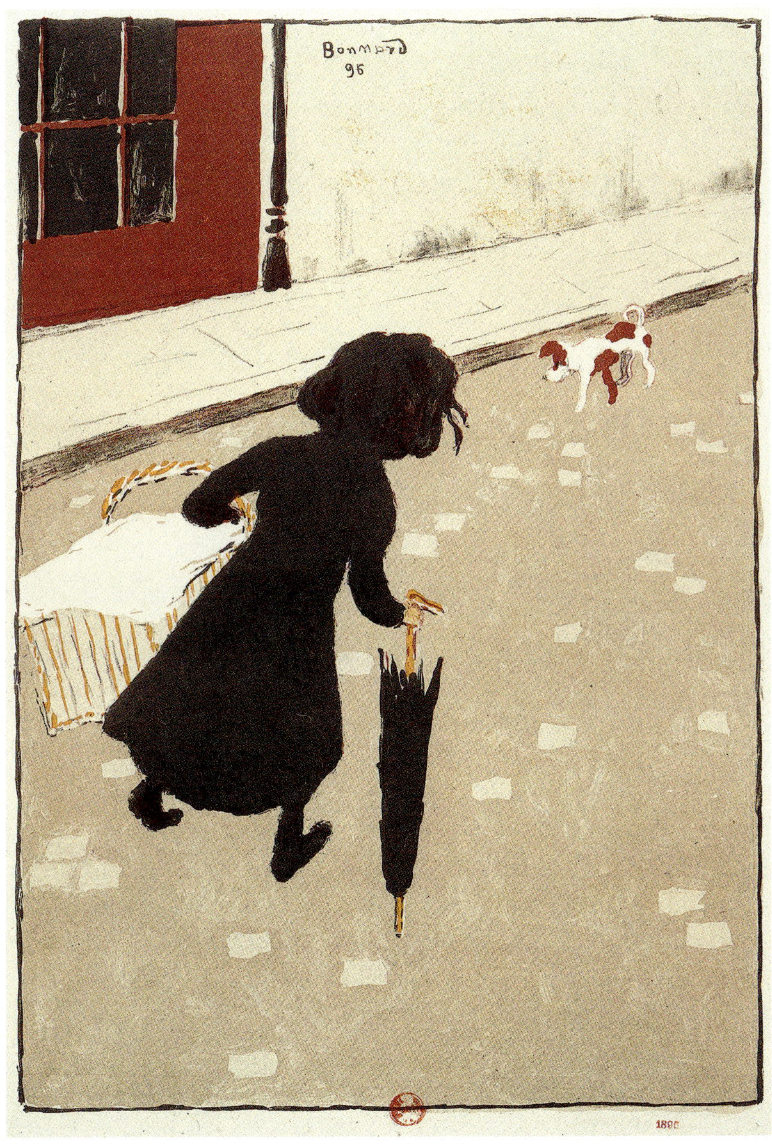
Bonnard
96
1896

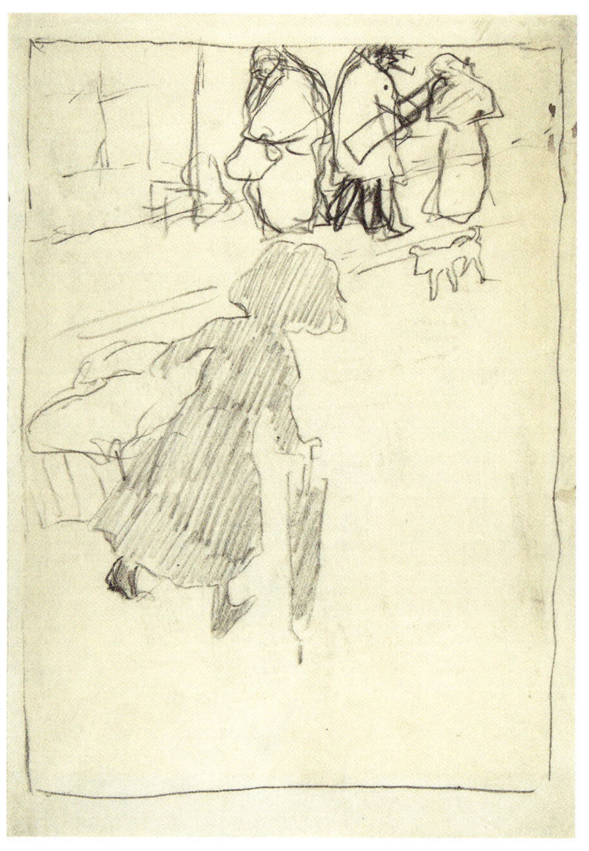

La Petite Blanchisseuse, 1895, pencil on paper, 31.2 × 21 cm. New York, The Metropolitan Museum of Art

Cats and dogs

“Animals do not merely play a secondary part in Bonnard’s output,” wrote Claude Roger-Marx in 1947. “The eyes of his basset and of his cat encapsulate all forms of loyalty, betrayal, and sorrow.” The eminent critic forgot to say that their role did not solely consist in expressing those feelings through potent silences. How could one imagine Bonnard’s great nudes of Marthe, lovingly modeled around 1900, without their legions of kittens, sleepy after love-making, terribly restless before? They were not the only ones associated with lewdness, however. Melbourne’s *Le Sommeil*—the slumber depicted related to what either precedes or follows the lover’s embrace—yields to the viewer’s fantasies with a sensuality that Natanson and Apollinaire likened to Renoir. The work was soon acquired by Gertrude Stein, who exhibited it in Rue de Fleurus among her Picassos and Matisses. These artists were too serious to frolic to the same extent as Bonnard, who had—let us not forget—provided licentious illustrations for Verlaine’s poetry collection *Parallèlement* at the beginning of the 20th century. And yet, at the foot of the bed where the brazen young woman—a sort of early Lolita—is resting, a small dog is lying down, facing the opposite direction. Like the cat in *L’Indolente* (1899), he is wearing a charmingly tied ribbon around his neck. Too well-behaved to be entirely honest, he is there to remind us of the erotic charge that dogs can embody on certain occasions, despite being a symbol of perfect domesticity in *The Arnolfini Portrait* by Van Eyck. As we shall see, there would be several of those occasions before Bonnard’s death. These potentially licentious dogs—depraved even, according to the Cynics of Antiquity—scarcely resemble the ones featured in *L’Après-midi bourgeoise*, who are aping their petrified masters. Final stages of digestion or Sunday boredom, we shall never know. But what eloquence in the forced motionlessness of those fearless hunters, with their sphinxian profiles!

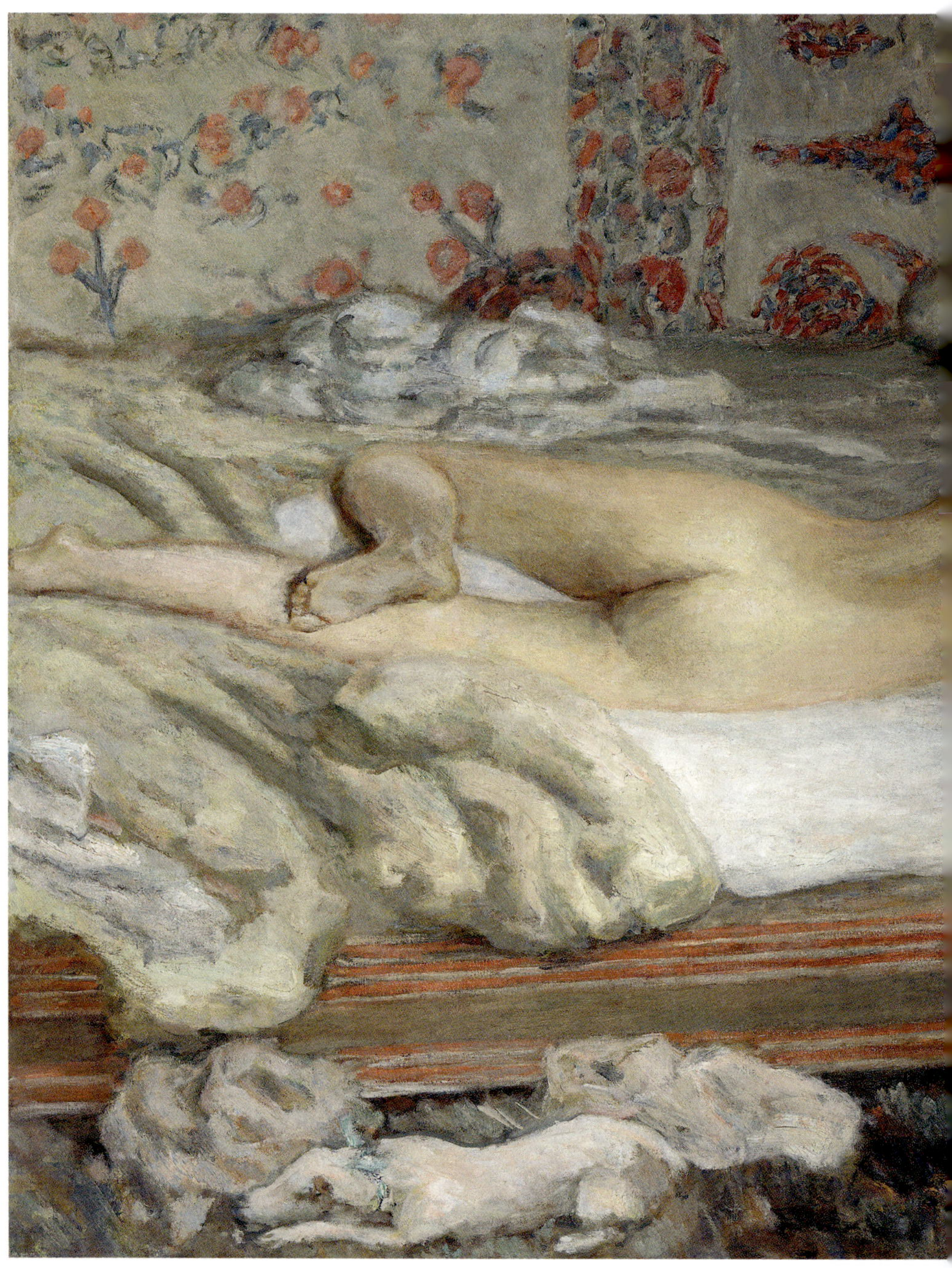

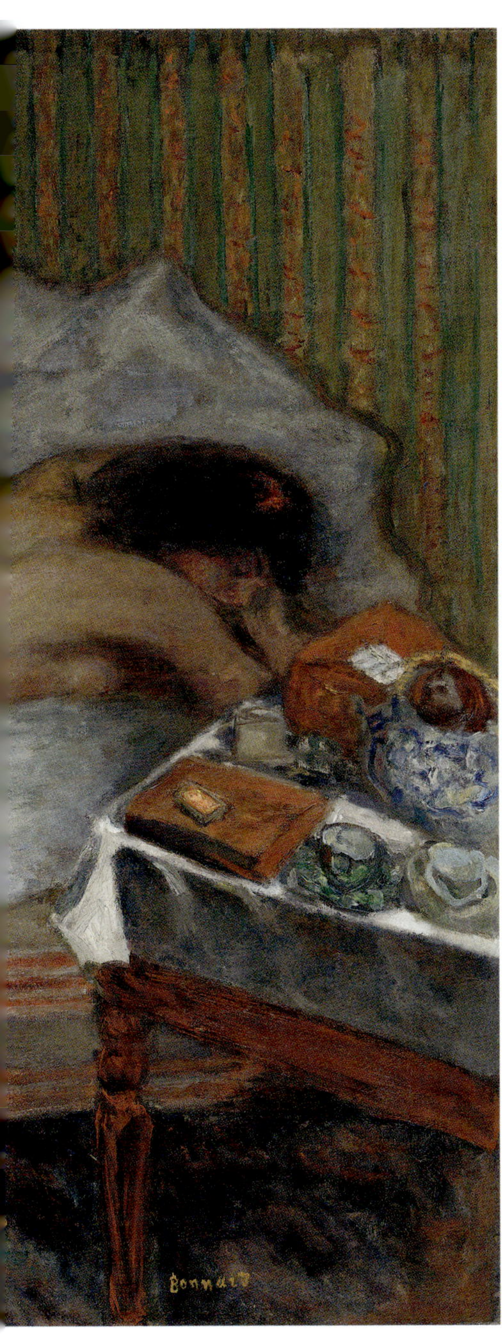

Le Sommeil, 1900, oil on canvas, 109 × 132 cm.
Melbourne, National Gallery of Victoria

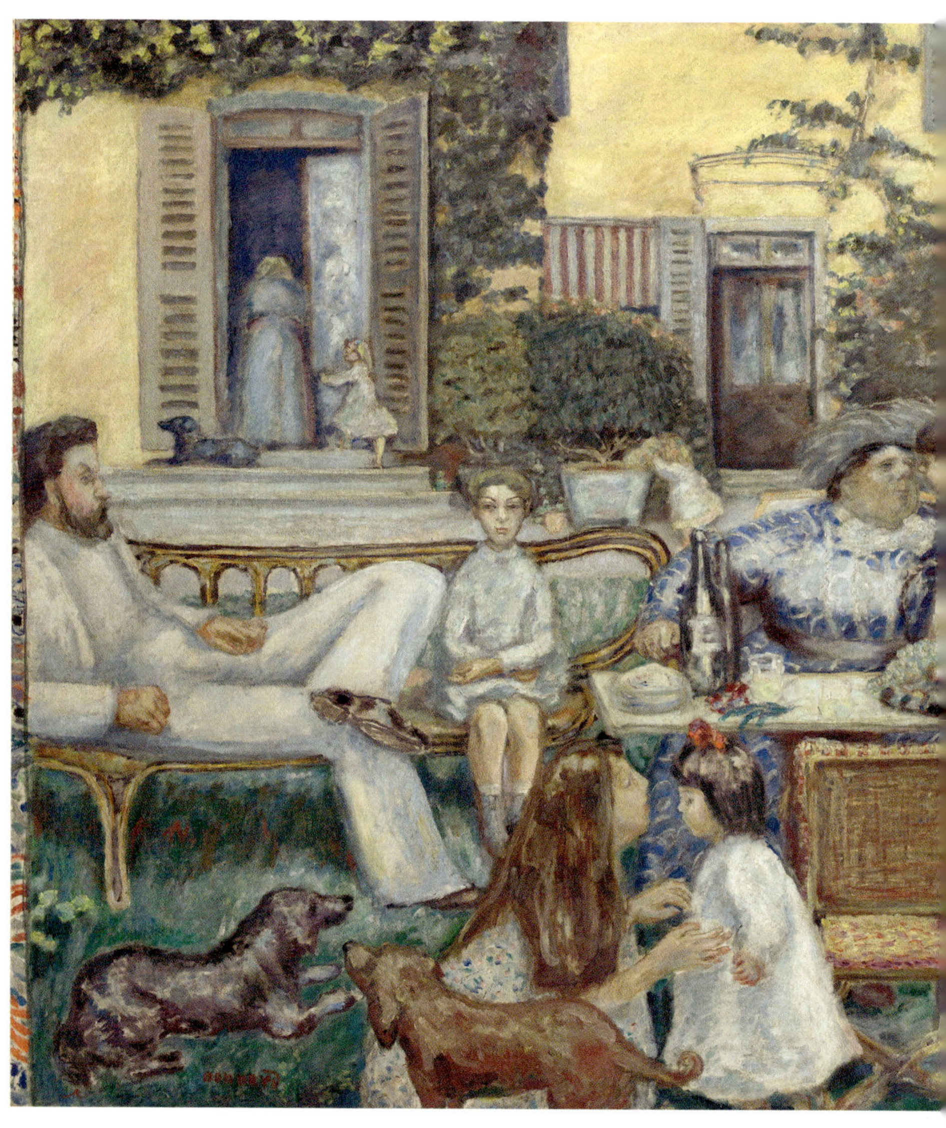

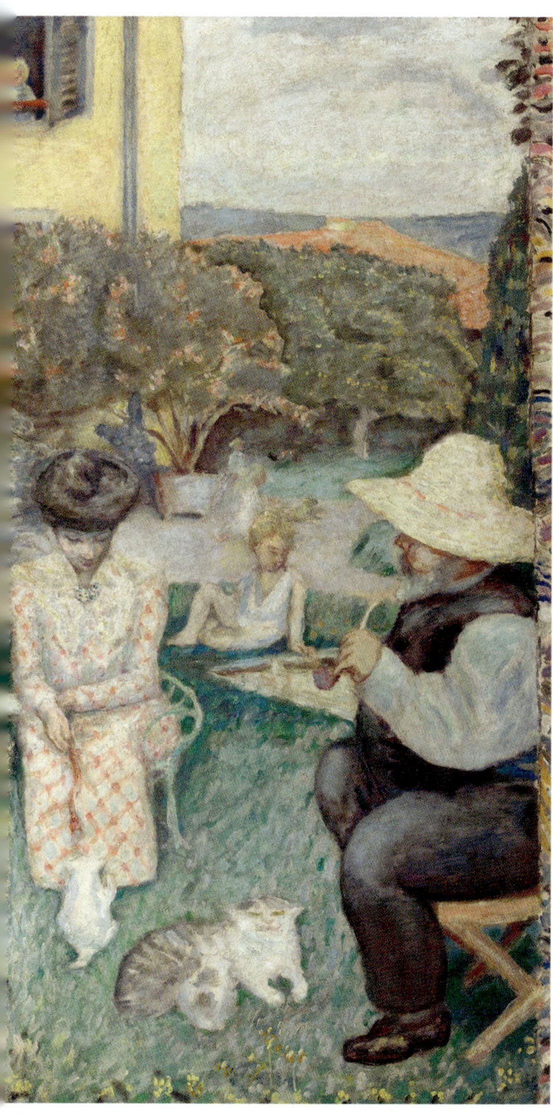

L'Après-midi bourgeoise, 1900, oil on canvas, 139 × 212 cm. Paris, Musée d'Orsay

Answer to Lautrec

This hunting theme provides us with a transition, as we turn to one of the major literary encounters in the field of illustration. Bonnard had already had some experience with the genre when the publisher Flammarion tasked him with illustrating *Histoires naturelles* by Jules Renard, who introduces himself to readers as a hunter of images who simply uses his eyes. The collaboration between painter and writer was no doubt a friendly one, even though Renard's diary doesn't mention him or their partnership. By agreeing to illustrate the book with 67 pen drawings, a technique which required a swiftness well-suited to the spontaneous character of these animal portraits drawn from life, the painter was facing two challenges: to respect the text's emotional and caustic simplicity, and to distance himself from what Lautrec had done previously. Five years had gone by since the edition illustrated by Toulouse-Lautrec, five years during which Bonnard had made a name for himself before consolidating his status by way of a contract with the Bernheim-Jeune gallery in 1906. To compare both books is to highlight the overrepresentation of dogs in Bonnard's images. The cover of *Histoires naturelles*, with its charming couple, provides one occurrence, and dogs return later, twice. First, there is the chapter that Jules Renard devotes to dogs, after swans and before cats. Taking place during a freezing winter, it tells the story of Pointu, who has only been given a small space under a roof that provides poor shelter.

Page 43

Jules Renard, *Histoires naturelles*, Flammarion, 1904, p. 70

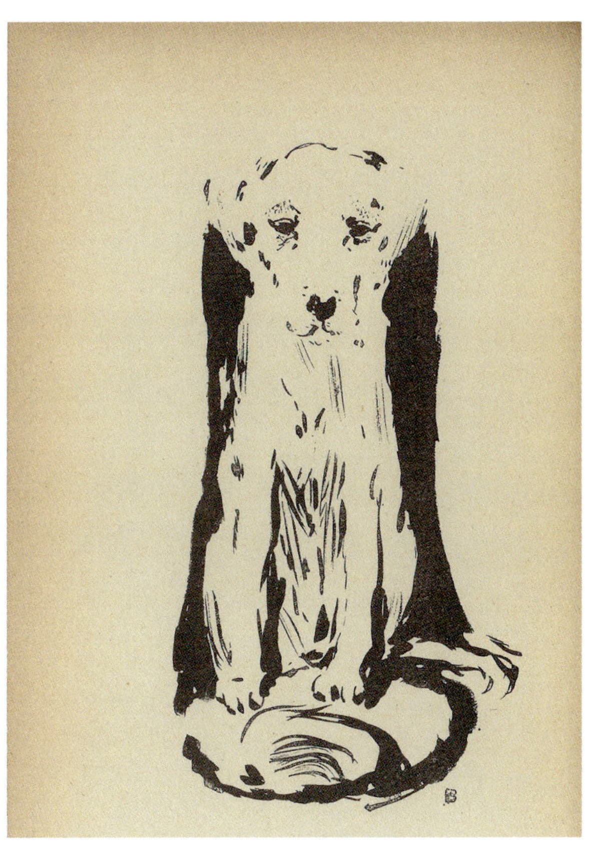

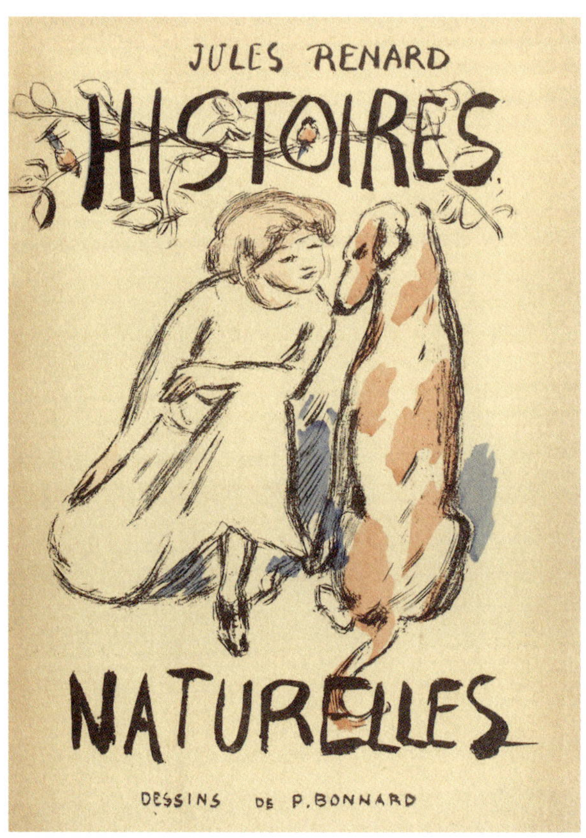

Page 45

Jules Renard, *Histoires naturelles*, Flammarion, 1904, front cover

Toulouse-Lautrec, *Histoires naturelles*, Floury, 1899, n. p., illustration for chapter titled "Le chien"

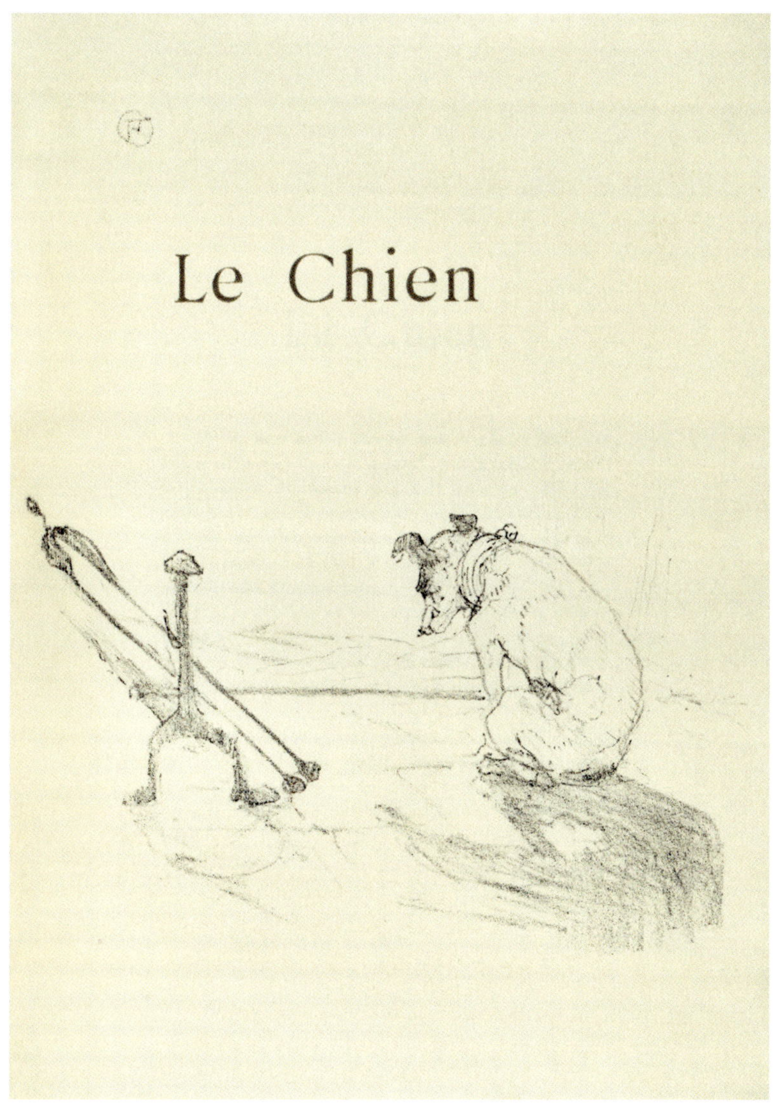
Le Chien

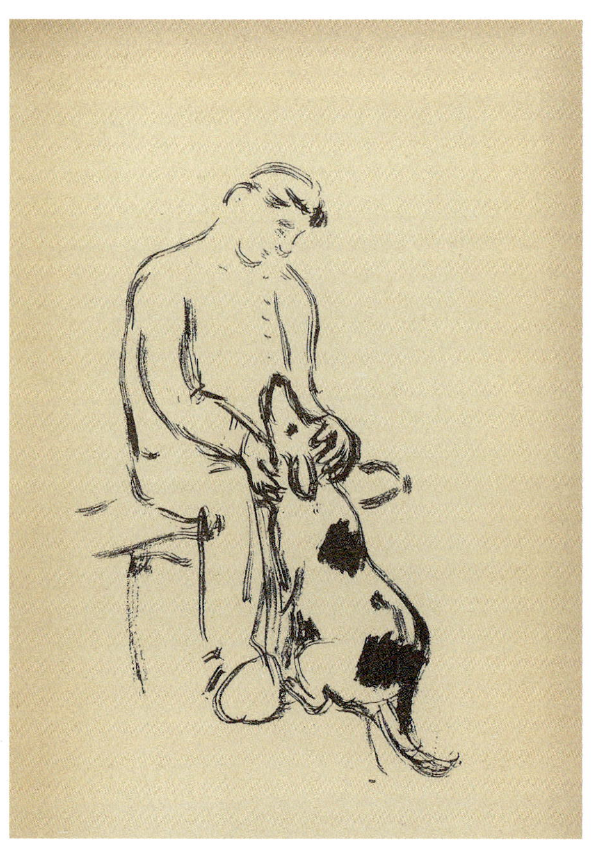

Jules Renard, *Histoires naturelles*,
Flammarion, 1904, p. 333

Reduced to smoldering on the family hearth, he resigns himself to his fate: “At a time when the teeth of stray dogs are chattering with cold, Pointu, nice and warm, with singed coat and baked backside, refrains from howling and laughs bitterly, tears in his eyes.” To illustrate human ingratitude, Lautrec had represented the dog from behind, his tail between his legs, concealing his sadness. On the contrary, Bonnard’s dog, who has Black’s features, shows us his downcast expression. No need for long speeches. The image even surpasses the very book it was meant to serve. Before the ending, Bonnard slips in his most poignant sketch. The hunt is over, and a man, Jules Renard’s younger double, is trying to explain the situation to his dog. They are both filled with the same regret at no longer being able to hunt for game, and each character is lost in the other’s gaze. The reader is struck by one particular detail, worthy of the pen and ink that drew it: the dog is wagging his tail, seeming to make the pen lines move. Despite being deprived of the pleasures of hunting, the dejected figure hasn’t lost his master. And that is well worth the woodcocks and partridges saved by the bell.

Pages 48–49

En bateau, 1910–1913, oil on canvas.
Toulouse, Fondation Bemberg

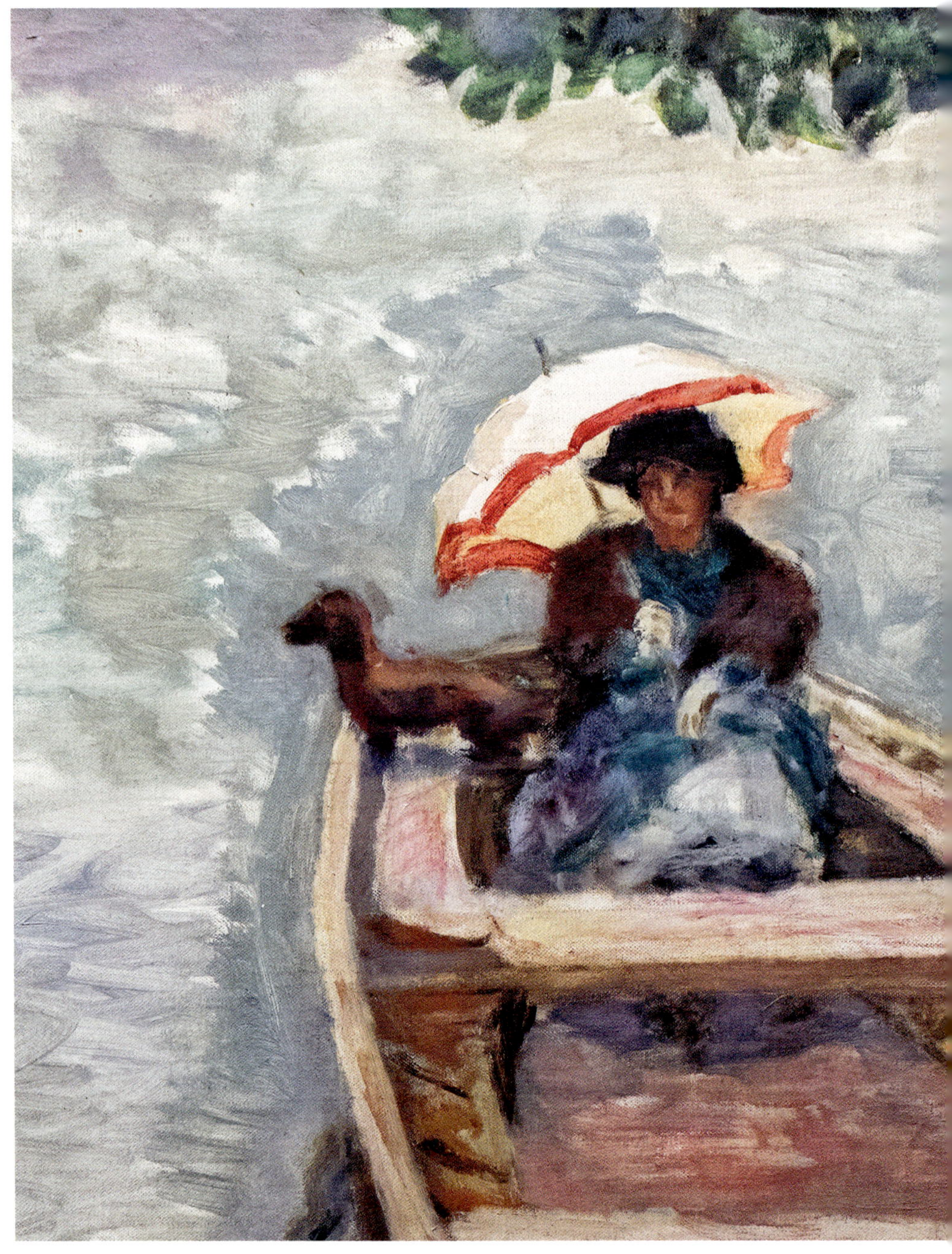

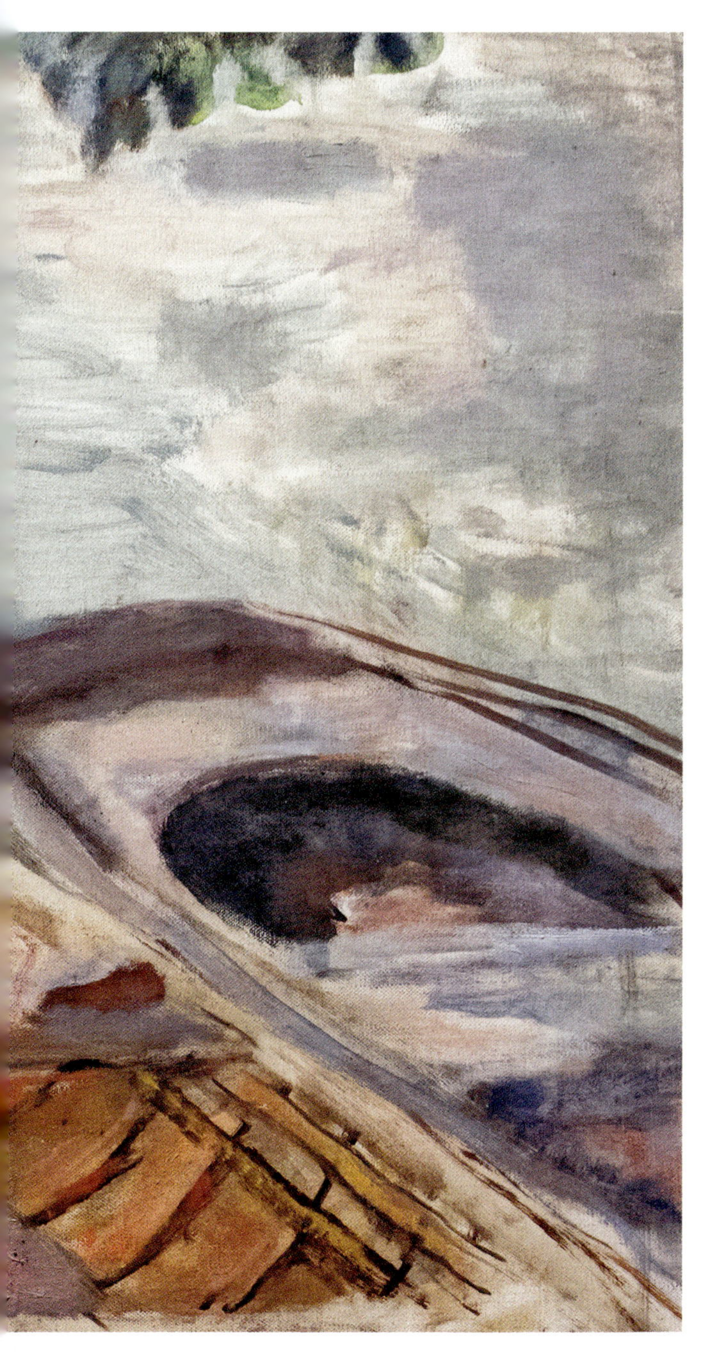

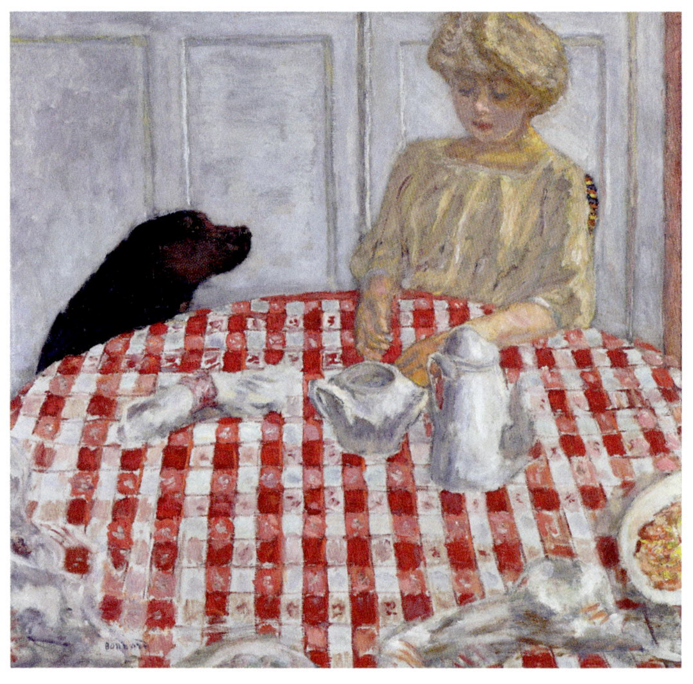

La Nappe à carreaux rouges or *Le Déjeuner au chien*, 1910, oil on canvas, 83 × 105 cm. Private collection

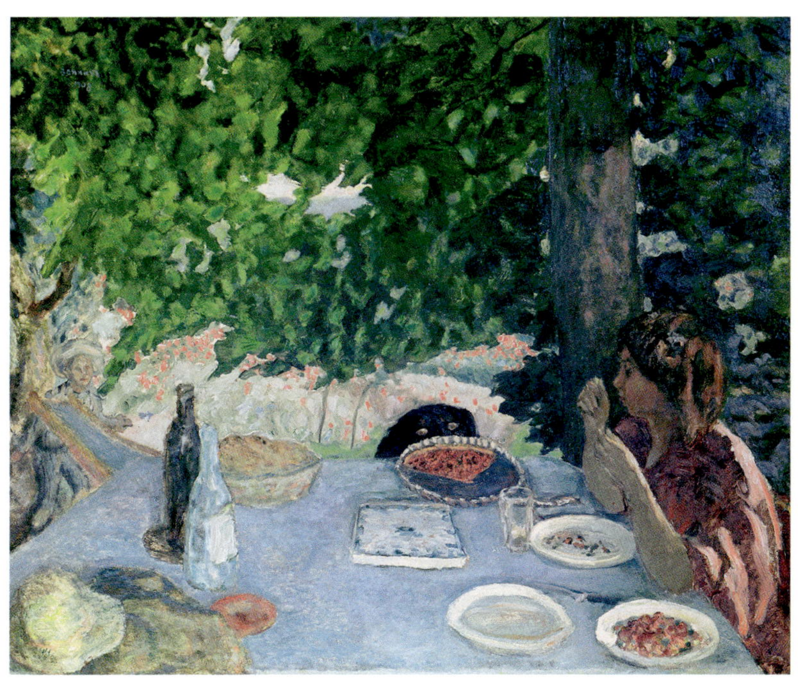

Le Gâteau aux cerises, 1908, oil on canvas, 115 × 123 cm. Germany, private collection

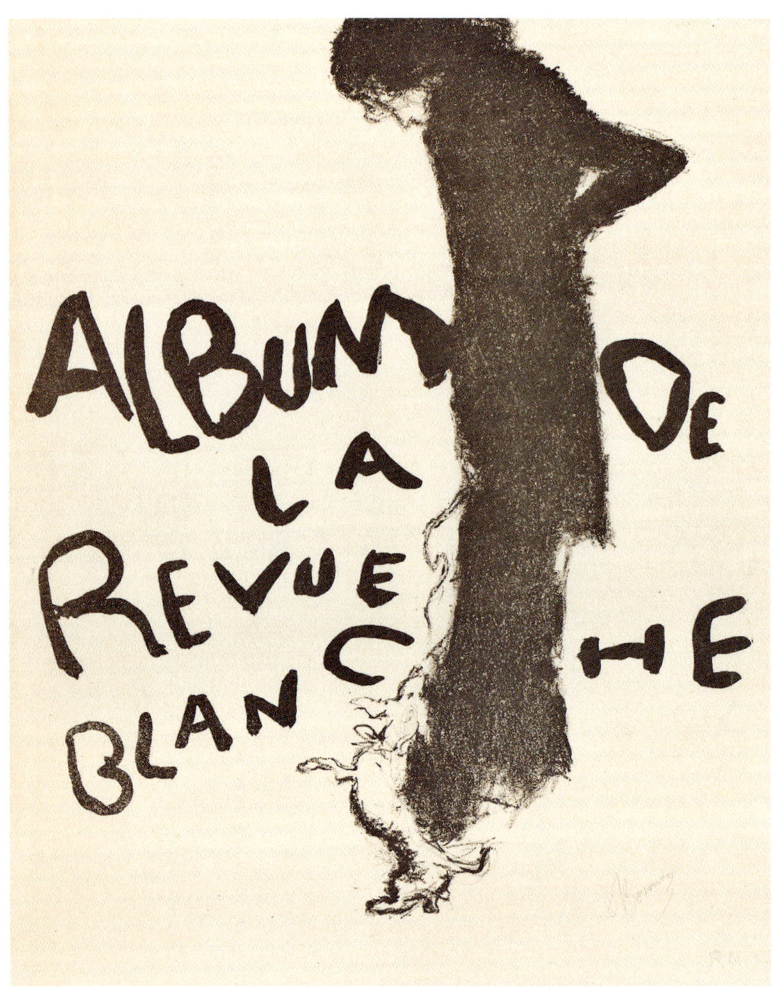
ALBUM DE
LA
REVUE
BLANCHE

"Avoir du chien"

Histoires naturelles did not claim status as a coffee-table book. On the contrary, the format, price, and mechanical reproduction of its illustrations aimed to reach a wide readership. Judging by the number of reprints, this resulted in success. Bonnard's altruistic view of art was satisfied, as was his literary talent. For lack of La Fontaine's *Fables*, which he had read with zeal (along with Verlaine and Mallarmé) and dreamed of illustrating, Bonnard displayed the fullest measure of his illustrative talent when he worked on the books of his friend Octave Mirbeau, another great lover of dogs and a tireless advocate for animal rights. There had previously been Verlaine's *Parallèlement* in 1900, with its soft pinks, ethereal prints and rare presence of a few bawdy yet elegant bassets. That a "lady" or a "girl" could have *du chien* (literally "something of a dog," i.e., a somewhat provocative charm), according to Verlaine, was enough to justify the canine metaphor. Illustrating Mirbeau, the witty but bitter critic of the Belle Époque era, called for more disturbing visual choices. Both men must have often met at the headquarters of *La Revue blanche* during the Dreyfus affair, which rallied them to action. A strange dog from Australia was always by Mirbeau's side during those militant times, a dingo who, provocatively and affectionately, had been given that very name. The name later became the title of a novel published in 1913, a dozen years after its hero's death.

Page 52

La Revue blanche, album cover, 1895.
Le Cannet, Musée Bonnard

Pages 54–55

Parallèlement, 1900, print, Ambroise Vollard publisher, n. p., "À Madame***"
double spread

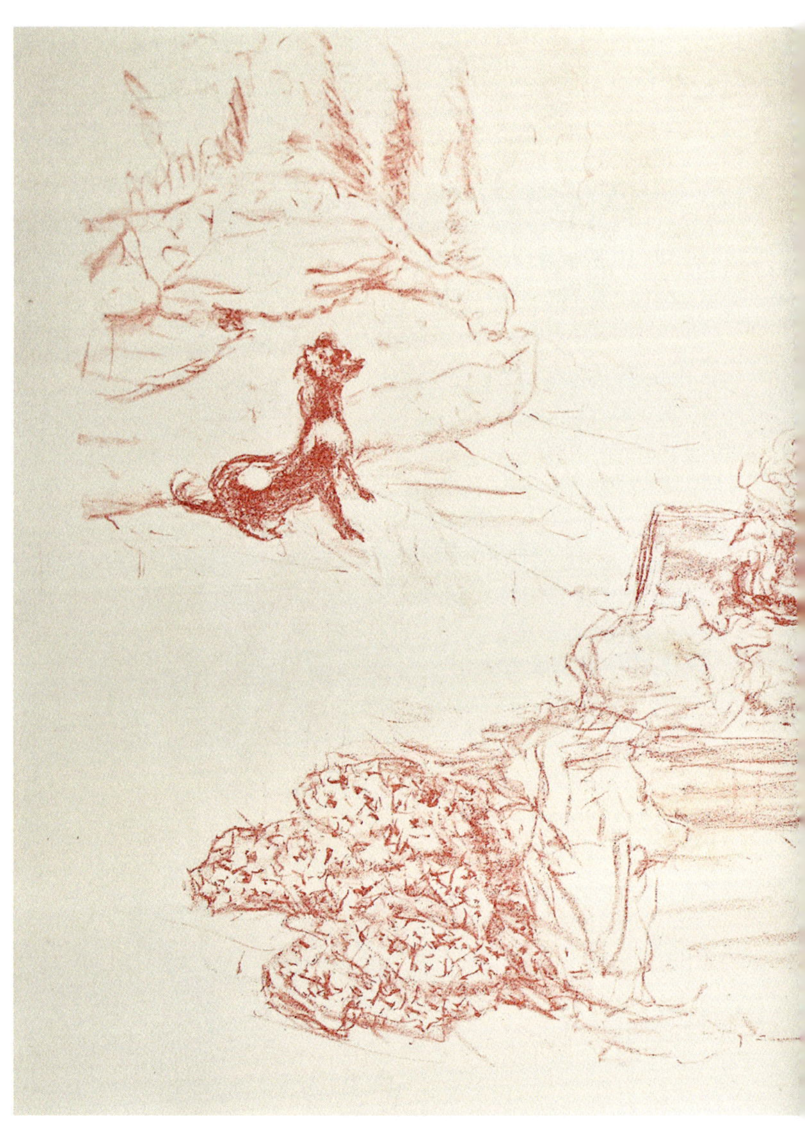

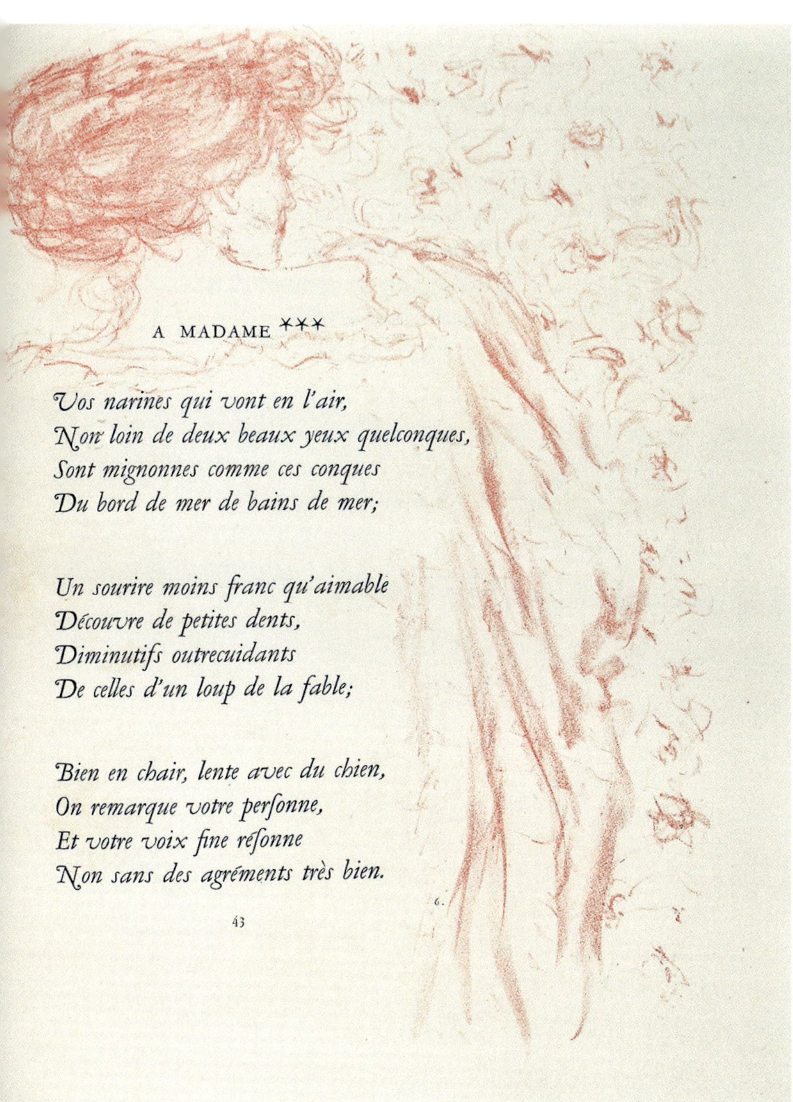

A MADAME ***

Vos narines qui vont en l'air,
Non loin de deux beaux yeux quelconques,
Sont mignonnes comme ces conques
Du bord de mer de bains de mer;

Un sourire moins franc qu'aimable
Découvre de petites dents,
Diminutifs outrecuidants
De celles d'un loup de la fable;

Bien en chair, lente avec du chien,
On remarque votre perſonne,
Et votre voix fine réſonne
Non sans des agréments très bien.

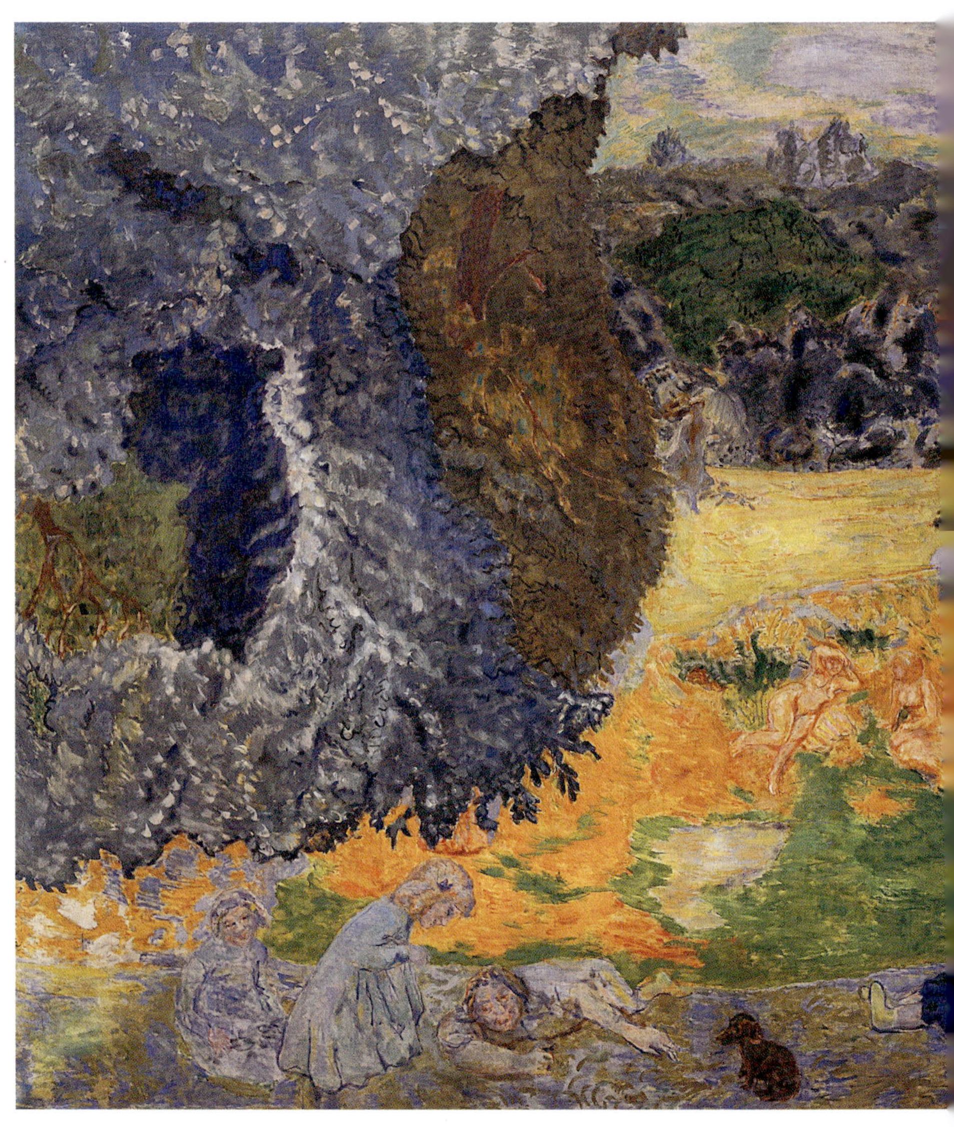

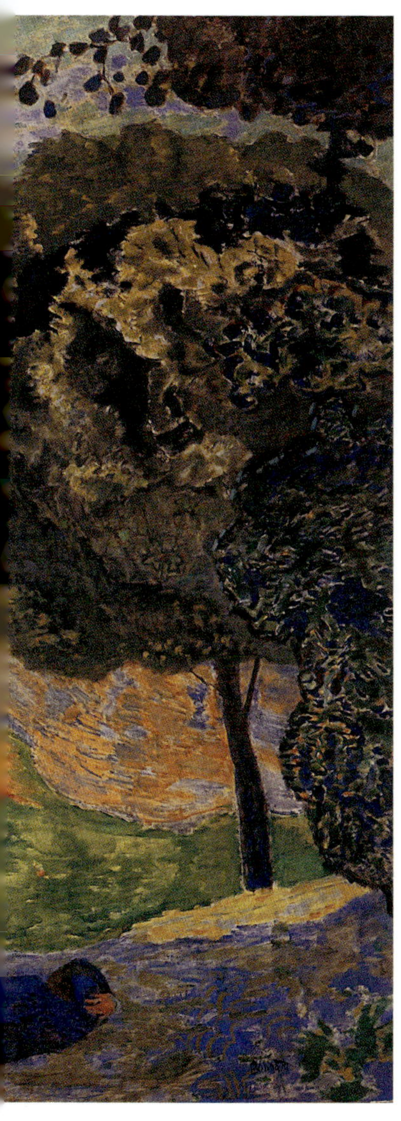

L'Été, 1917, oil on canvas, 260 × 340 cm.
Saint-Paul-de-Vence, Fondation Maeght

About ten more years would pass before Vollard, the publisher of *Parallèlement*, entrusted Bonnard with the task of giving a face and soul to the wolfish yet awfully endearing slayer of hens and sheep. The novel's genius stroke was to respect Dingo's ambivalence, as he veered from highly docile to completely wild, without a care for good or bad. Sometimes, he showed an awareness—an intelligence even—closer to humanity than might have seemed at first. Indeed, Bonnard resisted the temptation to draw overly anthropomorphic animals, as illustrators often did, giving his etchings a fearsome bite, to borrow a word from the language of engravers. The 1924 publication, falsely nonchalant, features masterful illustrations that shift from irony to pathos. Avoiding pretty, smooth, confined shapes, the images themselves bark out, so to speak. Three years later, *Les Histoires du petit Renaud* was published in collaboration with Léopold Chauveau, another lover of animals. The cover showed a child and a dog, both asleep. Was one the other's dream?

Page 59

Les Histoires du petit Renaud, Gallimard, 1927, front cover

LES HISTOIRES DU PETIT RENAUD

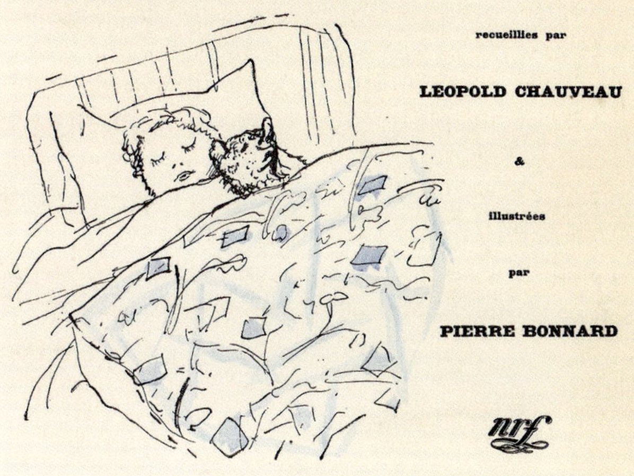

recueillies par

LEOPOLD CHAUVEAU

&

illustrées

par

PIERRE BONNARD

nrf

Librairie Gallimard

3, Rue de Grenelle - Paris

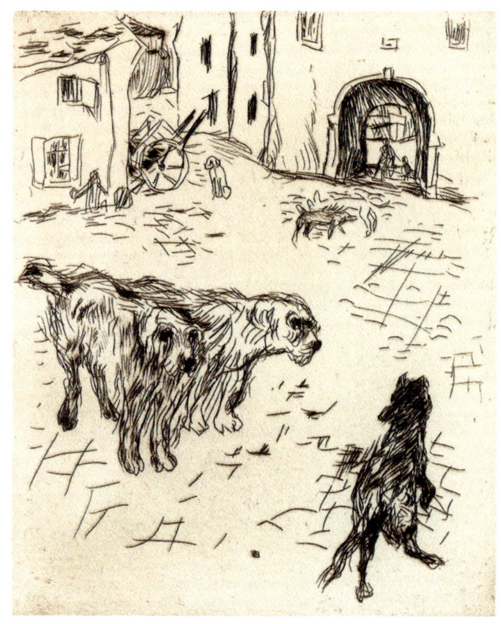

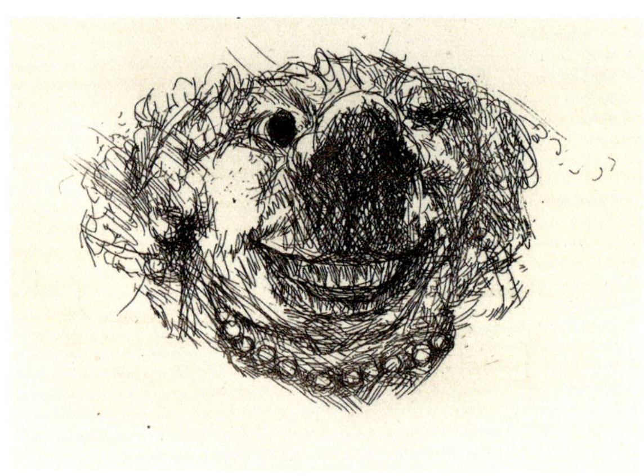

Dingo, 1924, etching, Ambroise Vollard publisher, plate titled “Tête souriante de Dingo,” p. 27

Dingo, 1924, etching, Ambroise Vollard publisher, p. 67

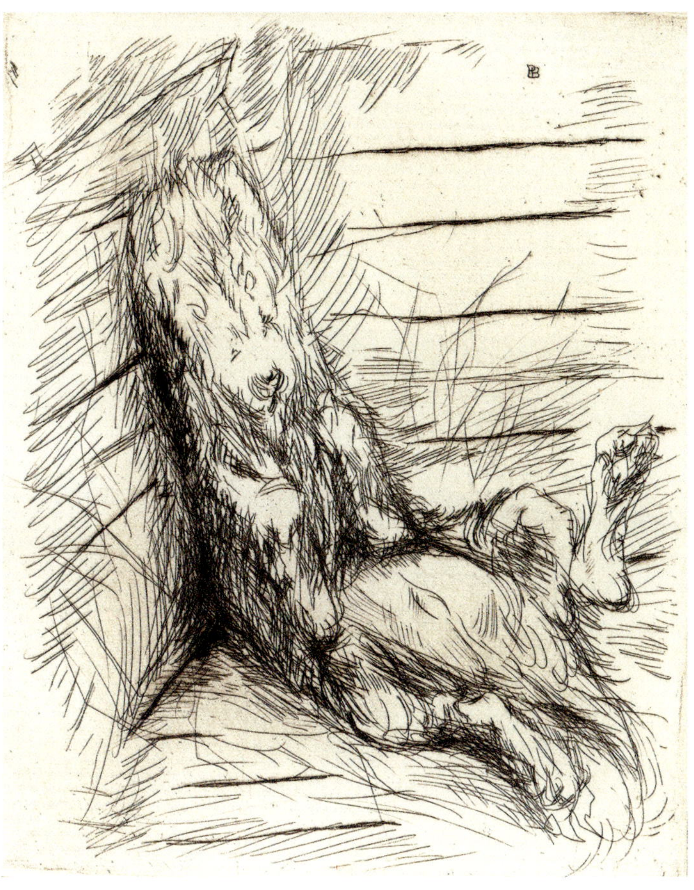

Dingo, 1924, etching, Ambroise Vollard publisher, plated titled "Dingo dans sa caisse," p. 8

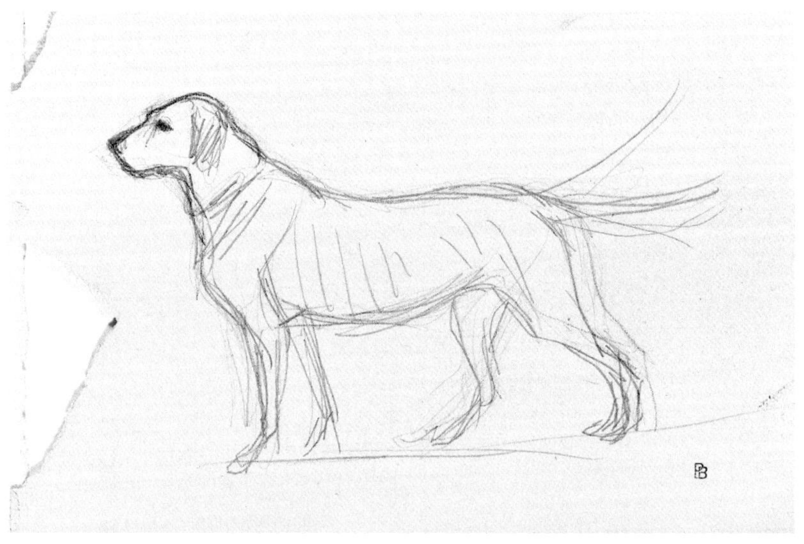

Chien, undated, drawing, 13 × 21.3 cm.
Paris, Musée d'Orsay (stored in the Musée du Louvre)

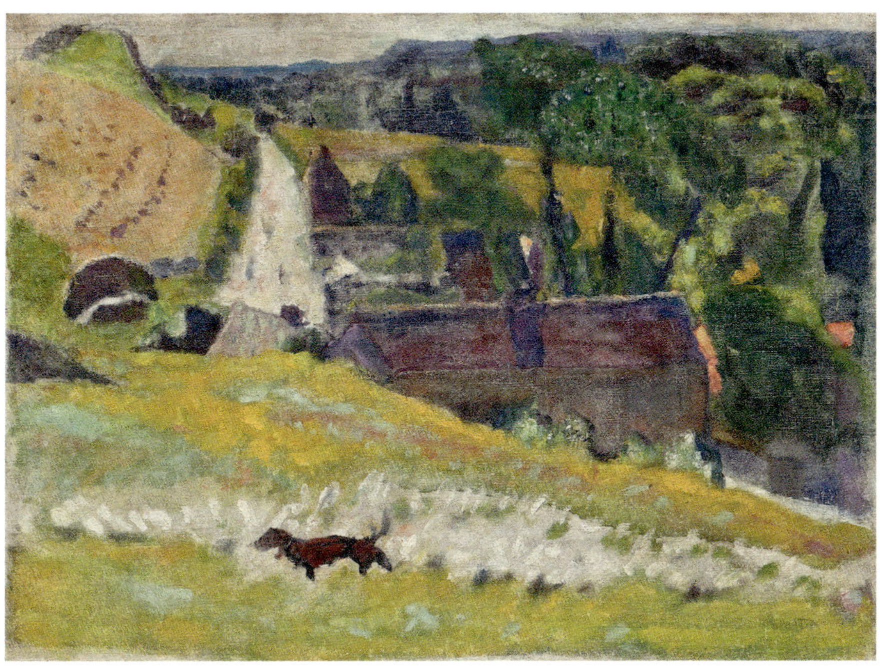

Paysage au basset, c. 1922, oil on canvas,
41,5 x 55 cm. Private collection

Marthe is no more

Mirbeau and Bonnard knew that we continually learn from the all-enveloping world driving us forwards. The painter's journals and notebooks are covered in a revealing shorthand, which goes from the day's weather to quick, indoor or outdoor sketches of humans and animals drawn on the spot. It's as if each note contained the whole world. The evidence being the countless representations of "women with dogs," as Bonnard puts it—women who somewhat resemble female centaurs. During the 1910s and 1920s, some of the bassets he chose to accompany Marthe or his mistress Lucienne Dupuy de Frenelle's magnetic presence were given legendary names, like Ubu and Poucette (the French name for Thumbelina). An amusing way of recalling his incursions into absurdist theater, his close friendship with Alfred Jarry, as well as that spirit of childhood so dear to Baudelaire, which Jarry and Bonnard both shared. As for tiny Poucette, the well-known character from the fairy tale by Andersen told by many a grandmother, she had to survive among others larger than her. The famous painting from the Philipps Collection, unusual for its psychological aspect, deserves all the praise it received at the Salon d'Automne in 1923, as well as its wide celebrity in the US. Marthe, taciturn as ever, is wearing a red sweater with white stripes which represent a kind of inner prison. The dog she is holding close to her chest has startled the painter, staring at him with its head to one side.

Page 65

Femme au chien, 1922, oil on canvas, 69.2 × 39 cm. Washington, The Phillips Collection

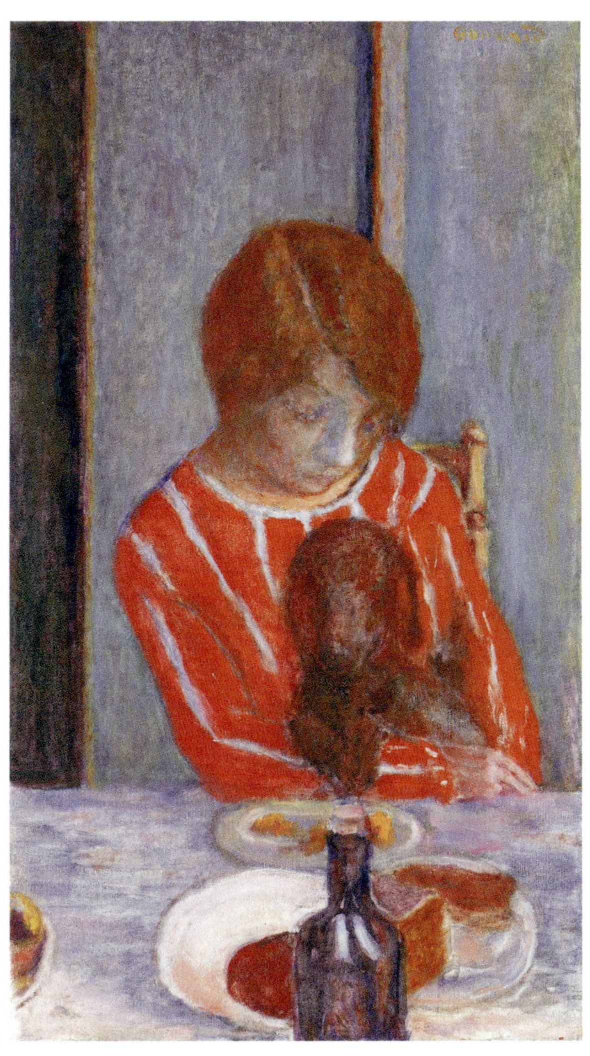

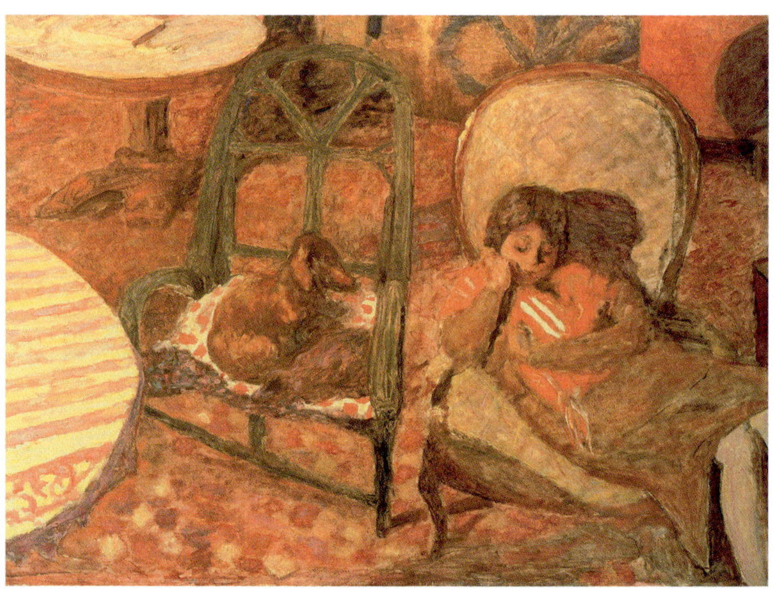

La Veillée, 1921, oil on canvas, 96.5 × 129.5 cm.
Private collection.

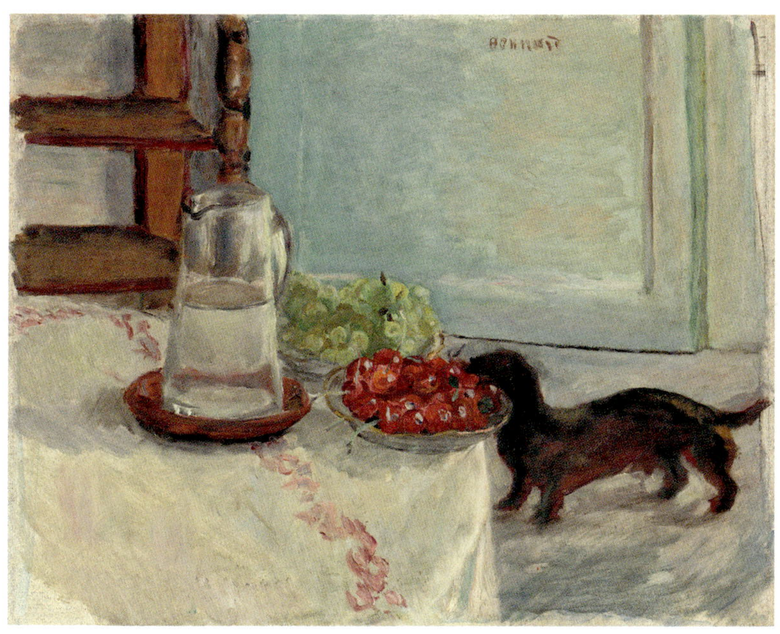

Nature morte au basset, circa 1912,
oil on canvas, 51.44 × 61.23 cm.
Washington, National Gallery of Art

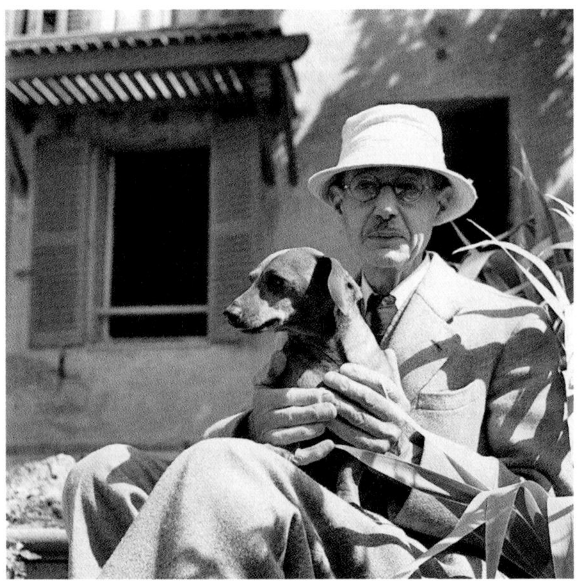

André Ostier, *Portrait de Pierre Bonnard*,
1941

The ever-returning bassets remain the discreet or invisible companions of everyday life, which they make more bearable. While they might not elevate us to their own level of nobility, they remind us, just as importantly, of our animal nature. Each painting seems to reveal some form of kinship with them. When Marthe died in January 1942, Bonnard is said to have confided to one of his pupils: "That is how life goes, we all have a bestial side that must be preserved for us to live, otherwise it would be the end, the end of the world." One of his last paintings is also one of his most visually intoxicating, perfectly suited to these words apt to constitute a philosophy of life. He painted it between 1940 and 1946, stopping and starting before entering mourning. To borrow from Mallarmé, whose works Bonnard often reread under the Occupation, Marthe the nymph, the Venus born of the ocean, but also Ophelia, had her life miraculously extended. Her entirely pink body seems incorruptible under Bonnard's loving gaze and his perpetually mischievous touch. The bathing water and the surrounding, all-encompassing blue are no longer distinct from each other. The white faience tiles radiate color—enchantment, so dear to Natanson, is in full bloom. Life and death appear to dissolve, as our gaze drifts about in weightlessness. Only the basset lying on the bathmat looks real, despite its heraldic function. The painter, *in absentia*, is watching us. Having become a dog, he is but silence and time.

Pages 68–69

Pierre Vuillard, *Portrait de Pierre Bonnard*, circa 1930–1935, oil on canvas, 114.5 × 146.5 cm. Paris, Musée d'Art Moderne

Pages 70–71

Nu au bain et petit chien, 1940–1946, oil on canvas, 122.4 × 151.45 cm. Pittsburgh, Carnegie Museum of Art

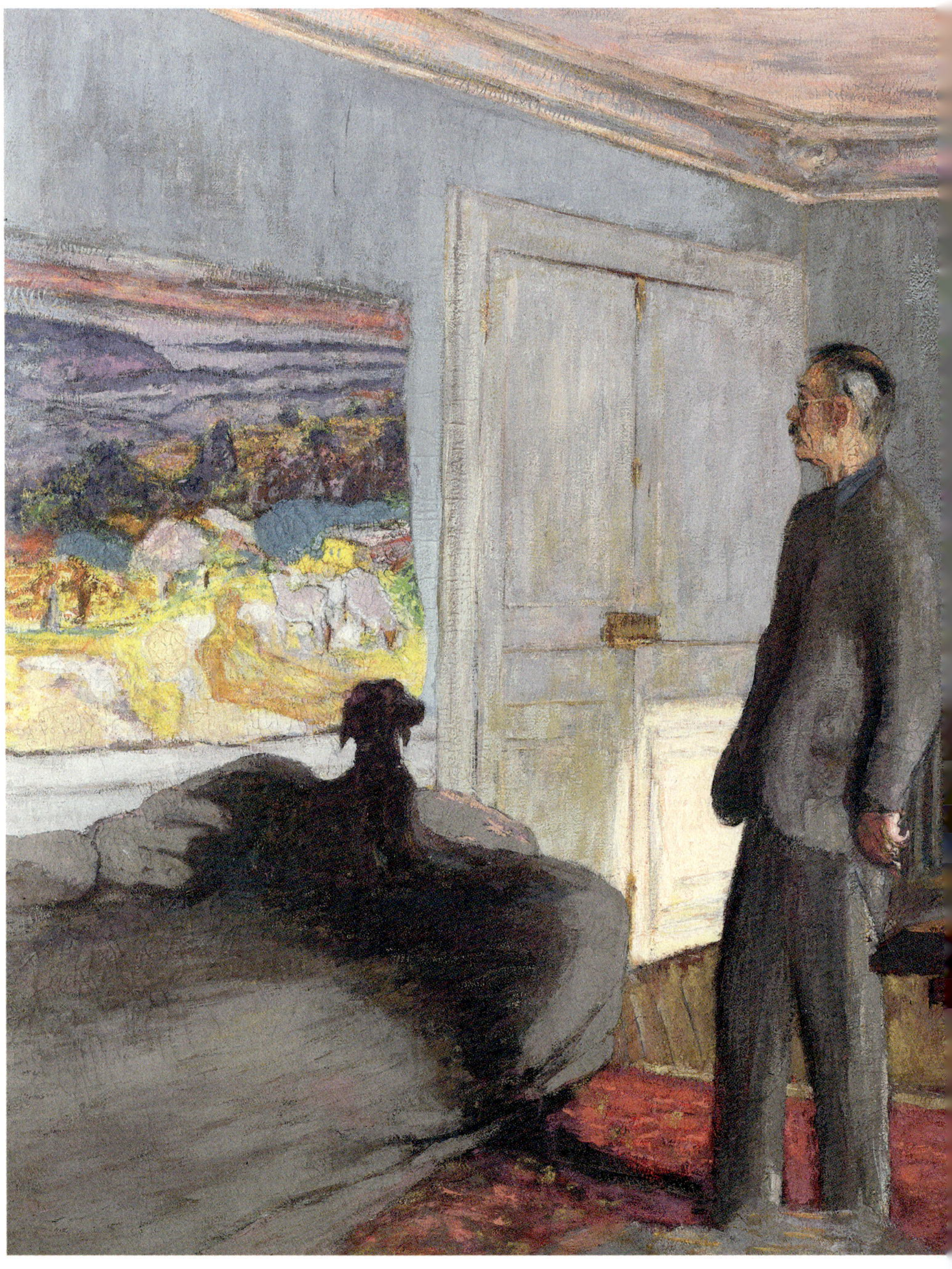

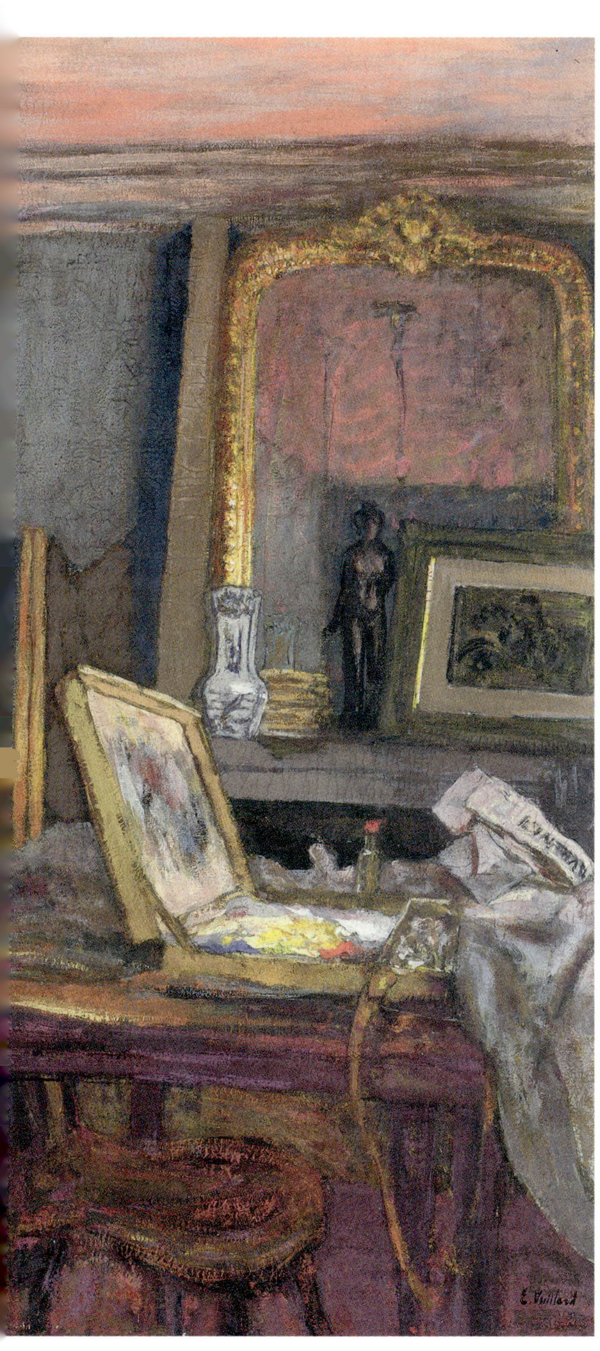
E. Vuillard

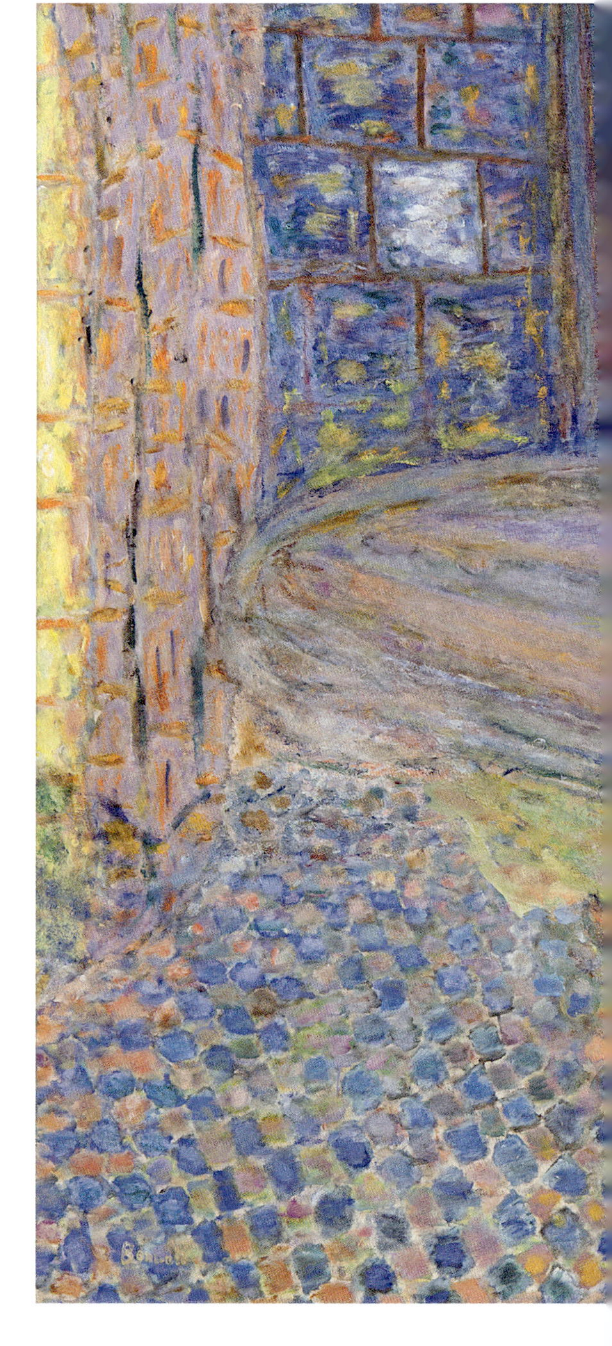

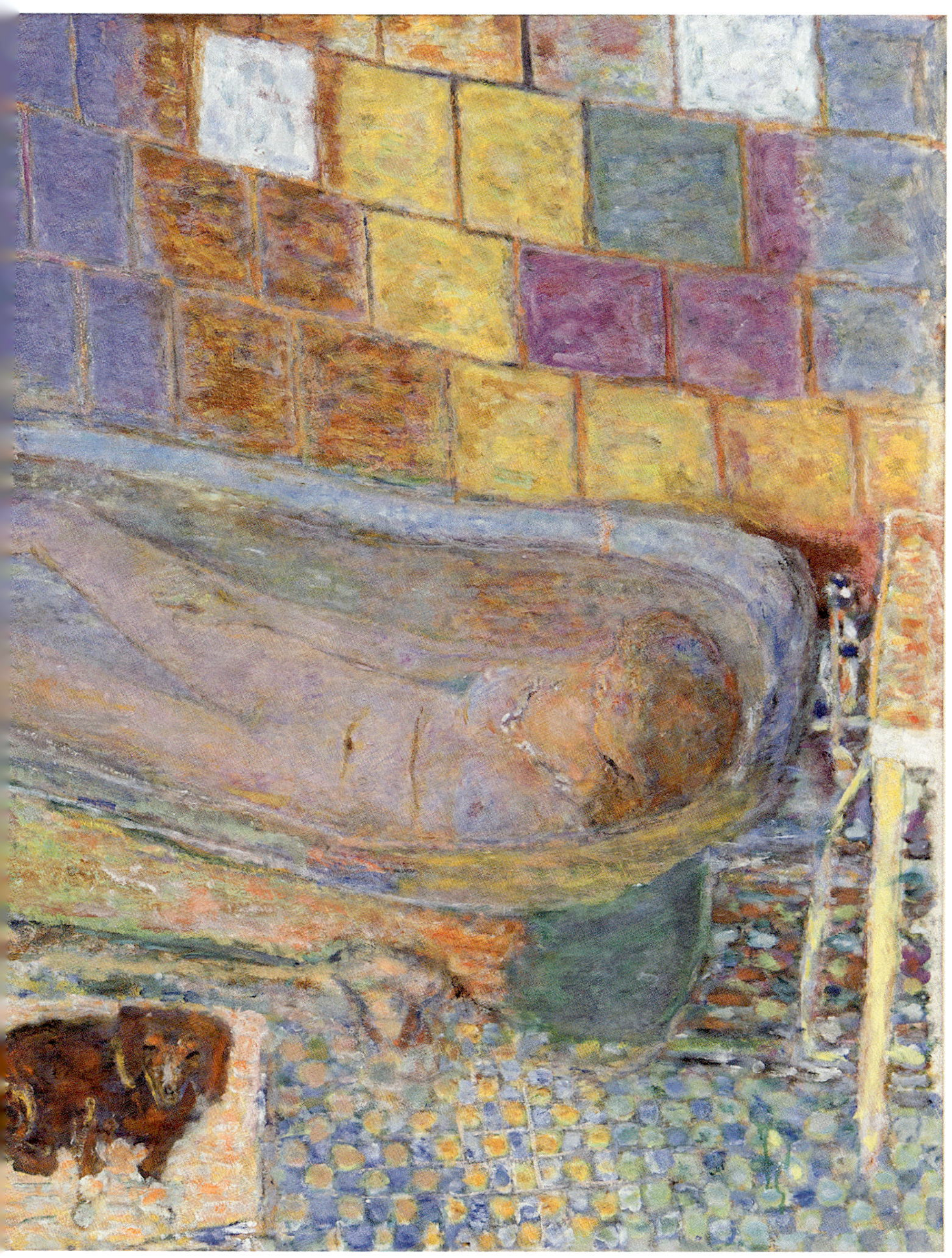

Pierre Bonnard's dogs

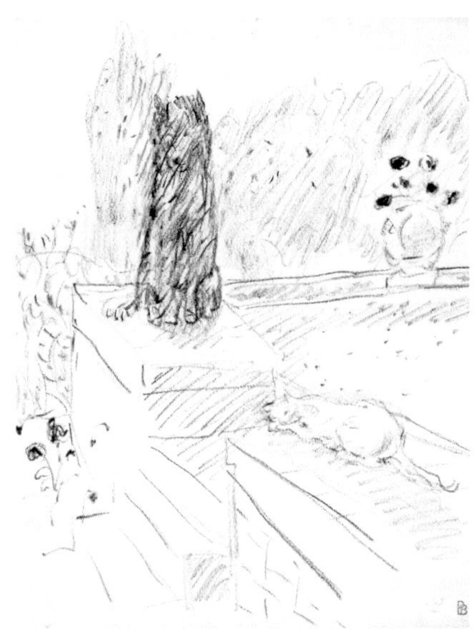

Dingo et la chatte Miche, 1924, lithographic drawing, 32.5 × 24.5 cm. Le Cannet, Musée Bonnard, on loan P.M.F.V.

Acknowledgements

Lou Clinton-Celini
Valérie Didier
Éléonore Guettat
Dominique Haïm
Peter Huestis
Carole Lenglet
Agnès Mulon
Véronique Serrano
Valeria Severini
Bertille Touchard
Cécile Verdier

This publication is supported by CHRISTIE'S

Photo credits

Couverture, 25. Southampton City Art Gallery/Bridgeman Images
1, 15, 16, 17, 62, 77. Musée d'Orsay, Dist. GrandPalaisRmn/Patrice Schmidt
11, 12, 52. Musée Bonnard, Le Cannet
14, 22, 23, 40–41. GrandPalaisRmn (musée d'Orsay)/Hervé Lewandowski
19. Mario De Biasi per Mondadori Portfolio /Bridgeman Images
21. 2026 The Clark Institute
26–27, 63. Christie's
29, 50, 51, 66, 70–71. Bridgeman Images
30, 31. GrandPalaisRmn (musée d'Orsay) /Gabriel De Carvalho
33. National Gallery of Art, Washington /Ailsa Mellon Bruce Collection
35. GrandPalaisRmn/Agence Bulloz
36. The Metropolitan Museum of Art, Dist. GrandPalaisRmn/image of the MMA
38–39. Courtesy of National Gallery of Victoria, Melbourne
48–49. Bernard Bonnefon. All rights reserved 2026/Bridgeman Images
54–55. Christie's Images/Bridgeman Images
56–57. G. Dagli Orti/NPL-DeA Picture Library/Bridgeman Images
65. The Philips Collection, Washington, USA/Bridgeman Images
67. National Gallery of Art, Washington /Collection of Mr. And Mrs. Paul Mellon
68. André Ostier/Association des Amis d'André Ostier
72–73. Carnegie Museum of Art, Pittsburgh, PA / Art Resource, NY
74. Musée Bonnard, Le Cannet /Frédéric Aubert
78–79. Fondation Henri Cartier-Bresson /Magnum Photos

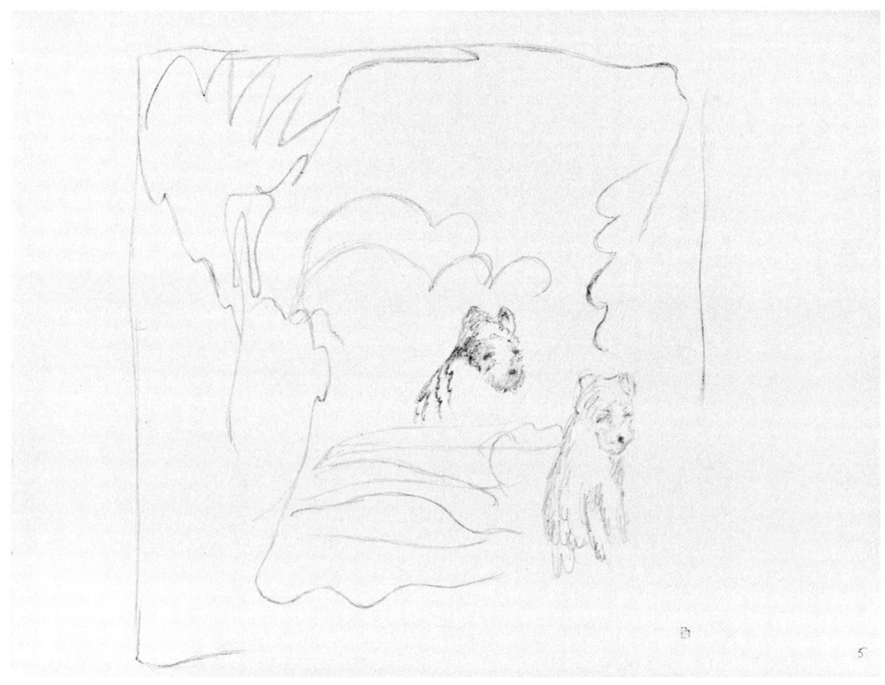

Pages 78–79

Deux études de chien dans un paysage, undated, drawing, 21 × 26.9 cm. Paris, Musée d'Orsay (stored in the Musée du Louvre)

Henri Cartier-Bresson, *Pierre Bonnard à son domicile, Le Cannet, France*, 1944

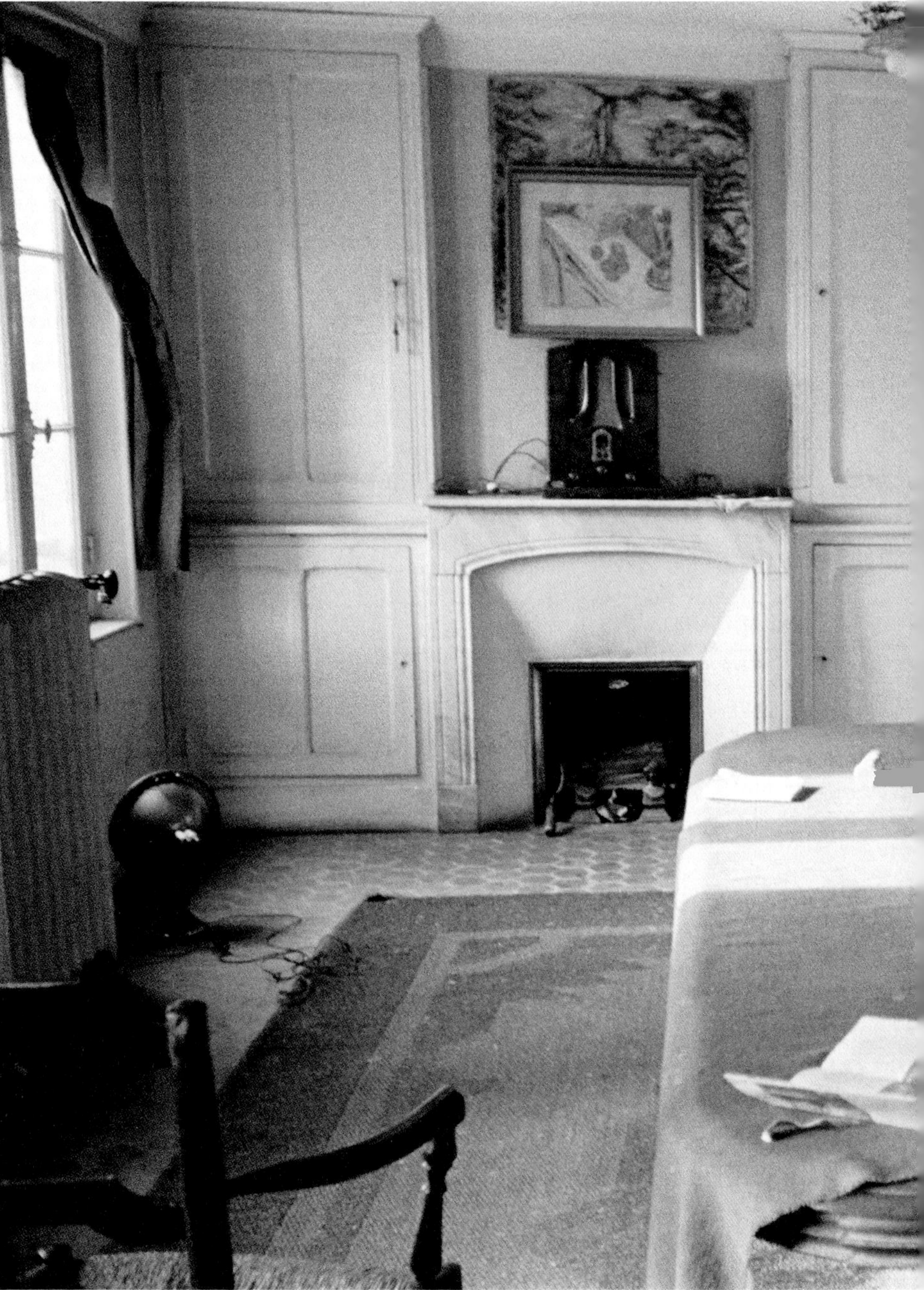

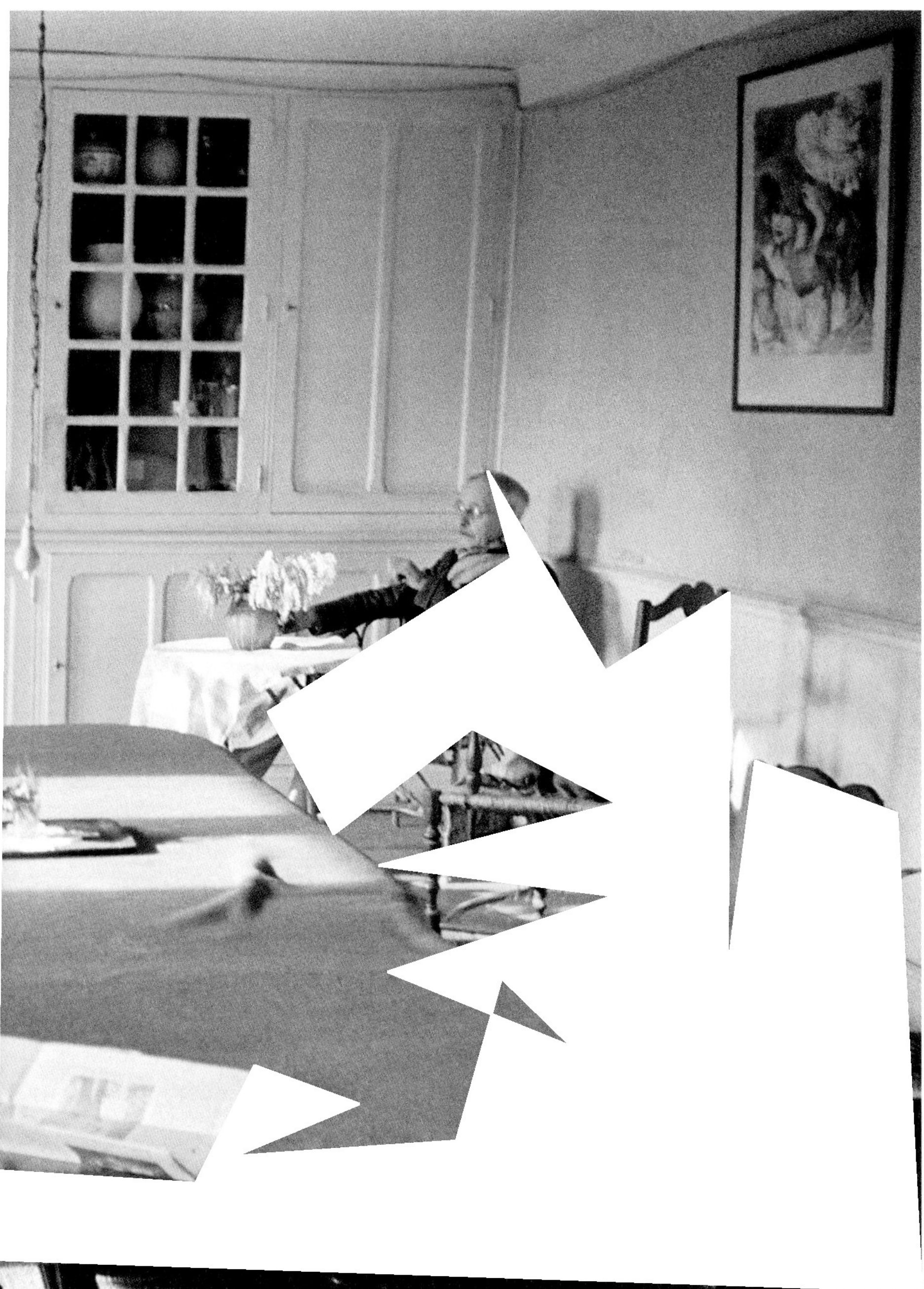

Forthcoming

William Wegman *and his dogs*
Andy Warhol *and his dogs*
Peggy Guggenheim *and her dogs*

Series editor
Martin Bethenod

Editorial coordination
Virginie Hagelauer
and Emma Gourault

Page layout
Annalisa Pagetti

Revision
François Grandperrin

Translation
Alexei du Périer

Proofreading
Ben Young and Helen Bell

Photo-engraving
Graphium

ISBN: 9782376661139

149, rue de Rennes,
75006 Paris, France
www.editions-norma.com

Printed in March 2026
by Livonia Print, Latvia

Cover: Bonnard, *Deux caniches* (detail),
1891, oil on canvas, 36.3 x 39.7 cm